MW00955030

Shadow Reflections Workbook

A guide to meeting and integrating your shadow

Written by: Sarah Satre

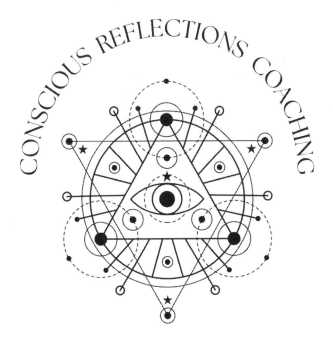

CONSCIOUS REFLECTIONS COACHING

Copyright © , Sarah Satre @ Conscious Reflections Publishing 2022
All rights reserved

The content contained in this book may not be reproduced, duplicated, or transmitted without direct permission from the author or publisher.

Under no circumstances will any blame or legal responsibility be held against the publisher or author for any damages, reparation, or monetary loss due to the information contained within this book, either directly or indirectly.

Legal Notice:

This book is copyright protected. It is only for personal use. You cannot amend, distribute, sell, quote, or paraphrase any part of the content within this book, without the consent of the author or publisher.

Disclaimer Notice:

Please note the information contained within this book is for educational and entertainment purposes only. All effort has been executed to present accurate, up to date, reliable complete information. No warranties of any kind are declared or implied. Readers acknowledge that the author is not engaged in the rendering of legal, financial, medical, or professional advice. Please consult a licensed professional before attempting any techniques in this book. By reading this document, the reader agrees that under no curcumstances is the author responsible for any lossed direct or indirect, that may be incurred as a result of the use of the informaiton contained within this document, including, but no limited to, errors, omissions, or inaccuracies.

Scan this QR code or go
www.consciousreflectionscoaching.com to access the
free masterclass and meditations that correspond with
this book and to check out my website and other
offerings:

This book is dedicated to my late parents David and Vickie. I am so grateful that they were mine... and to every person that has ever loved me in my life, thank you. I am honored, humbled, and forever changed. Thank you for reflecting back to me who I truly am.

Love, Sarah

Disclaimer

I created this workbook for people like you who are on a path of personal development and shadow integration. My true passion is coaching one on one and working intimately with people to help them uncover and integrate their shadow. I realize that personal coaching may be too much of a time and financial commitment for some, so it's my hope that this workbook can be the next best thing! While I believe that shadow work is one of the best tools we can use for personal development, I have to say that it is just a small part. After you uncover some of those deeper hidden emotions and aspects that you have repressed, it's so important to find a way to express or move through them somatically on a physical level as well. Our thoughts live in our heads and our feelings live in our body. True healing of the mind, body and spirit encompasses somatic practice and spiritual connection as well, so I highly encourage you to look into that. That is something we focus on in my programs, but there is also a wealth of knowledge online about somatic release. This workbook is about uncovering those parts of you that your subconscious mind has hidden away from you, but has managed to affect your conscious behaviors. Once you have uncovered these aspects, it's about taking radical responsibility to make the changes necessary to live a better life. Lastly, coaching and shadow work in no way is a replacement for therapy with a licensed doctor. If you are struggling with extreme mental disorders, suicidal/homocidal thoughts, I encourage you to seek a doctor or therapist.

Table of Contents

Welcome to Your Path Towards Shadow Integration!

CONGRATULATIONS to you for taking the brave step towards shadow integration and for investing in yourself! I am so proud of this workbook and I have full faith that it will change your life! Often times, what prevents us from advancing in life is our lack of awareness about what lies beneath our persona and how our shadow is affecting so many aspects of our life. I guarantee that if you take a little time each day to answer these journal prompts and really reflect on the things you learn about yourself, your life will change in so many ways. You will understand more why certain things trigger you, you will realize why your partner annoys you so much sometimes, and you will see why you might be continuing to attract toxic people, jobs, partners, or circumstances. By having this awareness of our shadow, we can begin to be freed from our intense emotions and respond to life with more grace. Remember this is your personal workbook. You and only you will see these answers... so dig deep and get real with yourself! Be brutally honest with your answers, but remember to be gentle with yourself. Often times, when we start to see how our shadow has affected our life and relationships, we can feel a little guilt or shame for our past behaviors. DO NOT succumb to the guilt spiral! Instead, give thanks for the awareness and the lessons. You are here and you are doing the work, so GOOD FOR YOU! I recommend that you make your journaling experience a sacred spiritual practice of beautiful self discovery and make sure that you have a safe place to keep your journal, so that you feel safe to completely let go and get raw and honest with yourself. This work requires a deep level of owning your so-called undesirable traits as well as being compassionate with them.

I recommend taking on this workbook a few journal prompts at a time, and really take your time reflecting on your answers and see what you can learn about your inner world. I also recommend beginning each shadow session with my Shadow Reflections Heart Opening meditation to prepare your mind, body, heart, and soul for this deep, transformative, and intense work. Please take your time, be intentional, and remember that shadow work can be intense, so be kind to yourself.

Now, it's time to roll up your sleeves get to work!

What is the Shadow?

The 'shadow self' is a concept first coined by the Swiss psychiatrist Carl Jung that describes those aspects of our personality that we learned to reject and repress into our unconscious that we don't like or because society, our community, or our family told us were bad. This includes our so called bad aspects as well as some good traits or hidden talents. For one reason or another, we decided that it was safer to deny those aspects than own or express them, so we repress them into the place that we call 'the shadow.' Although, we have denied these traits, they still live inside of us and they have needs that they are trying to get met through relationships in our everyday lives. Since, we are completely unaware of our unconscious shadow aspects and their needs, this happens without our conscious awareness, causing us to overreact when that shadow aspect becomes triggered. This is the cause for most of the disharmony in our lives. Our shadow aspects are, often times, those parts of us that need the most healing, and can cause us to subconsciously find back door or manipulative ways to have those needs met. That is why shadow work is such an integral part of experiencing and attracting healthy relationships and circumstances. Shadow integration is the process of learning about those shadow aspects and meeting their needs. It is not about getting rid of them altogether. If you want to learn more about the shadow, I have created a free masterclass on the topic of shadow work, as well as 5 meditations to correspond with this book. You can find them all on my website at www.consciousreflectionscoaching.com or scan the QR code at the beginning of this book. Please check them out!

Commit to your Bliss!

Before we get into the beautiful, messy, scary, transformative process of deep shadow work, let's take a look at why you are here, how comitted you are, and what you hope to gain from this process of self discovery and shadow integration.

1) What made you decide to commit to a path of personal development and growth?

_____

_____

_____

_____

2) On a scale of 1-10, how committed are you to a daily practice of self discovery and growth? Can you make time daily to answer a few questions from this workbook and really reflect on what you learn about yourself?

_____

3) What are a few things you are ready to change about your life today?

_____

_____

_____

_____

_____

4) What do you believe has held you back from creating your best life and accomplishing your goals?

_____

_____

_____

_____

5) Do you have any personal, spiritual, financial, or career goals that you are striving for at this time? If so, what are they? If not, I challenge to to set a new goal for yourself.

_____

_____

_____

6) Set an intention for what you hope to gain from completing this workbook.

_____

_____

_____

_____

7) On a scale of 1-10, how happy are you overall with your life currently?

_____

8) Do you feel connected to your higher self/soul or spirit?

_____

9) What is your daily self devotional or spiritual practice? Do you have a sacred space to practice? If you do not have a regular practice, I challenge you to start today and make the decision to devote time every day to personal and spiritual growth. Create a space that you can make sacred to visit daily for this practice.

_____

_____

_____

_____

Ok, let's get into it!

Understanding Your Persona

As we learned in the video presentation, Our Persona is the mask we wear for the world. It's often times how we identify who we are and our strengths. Answer the journal prompts below to help you to get a better understanding of your persona.

10) List 3 characteristics about yourself as a person and your personality that you are very proud of. Your most highly favored attributes about yourself.

_____

_____

_____

11) For each characteristic, I want you to think back to the first time either in your childhood, adolescence, or early adult life when you were catalyzed to embody that characteristic (for example: I am proud that I am independent. I had to become independent because my parents were always at work and didn't make much money so I had to take care of myself and provide for myself at a young age.)

_____

_____

_____

_____

_____

_____

12) Do this for each positive trait that you identify with and spend some time in contemplation acknowledging how each quality was born. Try to imagine at what exact moment did you decide to embody that trait.

_____

_____

_____

_____

_____

(**Heres's an example of how to do this exercise)

My 3 qualities

- Resilient ~ I had to become resilient when my mom died.
- Independent ~ I had to work since I was 14 and take care of myself.
- Considerate/ sweet ~ I learned when I was a little girl that if I was sweet and considerate, I would make people happy and receive love and attention.

13) Were these qualities born from a time when you experienced a challenge to overcome? If so, what was the challenge? Were these qualities born to keep you safe or to receive love? Or, do you naturally posses these qualities?

_____

_____

_____

_____

_____

14) Do you ever feel like you have grown tired of being that person that is embodying those qualities all the time? Do you ever find yourself wanting to be the complete opposite? (This can happen when we srongly identify with our persona; for example: I am tired of always being independent. I would like to be able to relax and let someone take care of me.)

_____

_____

_____

15) If so, how does this thought of letting go of those qualities on occasion make you feel? (e.g. the thought of being less independent and more irresponsible is exciting to me, and it would give me relief.)

_____

_____

_____

_____

16) If you answered yes to those questions, how can you find healthy ways to incorporate that desire into your life? (that desire is just your shadow aspect wanting to have a need met. For example: I could take a personal day for myself on occasion or I could ask for help more and allow myself to rely on others more in a healthy way. This is shadow integration.)

_____

_____

_____

_____

17) How would your friends and family describe you as a person? How do you feel about that?

_____

_____

_____

_____

_____

18) Would you say that those qualities you listed that you are proud of is why your friends, family, or romantic partners are attracted to you?

_____

19) Do you ever feel pressure to maintain these qualities to keep people in your life or to live up to their expectations of you?

_____

20) How do you feel when you see people being the opposite of your 3 qualities (from question #10) that you are proud to embody? (e.g. I am proud to be independent, therefore, I am turned off by people who can't take care of themselves and rely on other people, or who are irresponsible.)

_____

_____

_____

_____

_____

_____

21) When you see other people embodying those same desirable traits you are proud to embody, are you more attracted to them?

_____

22) What would you like to be most recognized for? Are any of those qualities that you are proud to embody on that list?

_____

_____

_____

23) Who would you be without those qualities that you listed that you are proud of? What other positive traits could you foster and grow?

_____

_____

_____

24) Do you ever feel guilt or shame if you are not embodying those qualities that you take pride in?

_____

25) Do you feel obliged to be that person or fear disappointing people if you do not embody those traits? If so, why?

_____

_____

26) Who do you admire or look up to? What do you admire about them?

_____

_____

_____

_____

27) How can you take action to be more admirable?

_____

_____

_____

_____

Take some time to read over and reflect on your answers. Most likely, those qualities that you are proud of are what you've created as your persona. It's important to remember that our persona is a part of who we are and not just a 'Mask' we wear. We don't want to invalidate these qualities we love about ourselves, we just want to get a deeper understanding of what is beneath those qualities and why we decided to identify with them so strongly. We can also have certain contradictory qualities that we tend to embody at different times or with different types of people or different environments as well. For example: prior to my shadow integration, I was proud that I was very responsible at work, but in my personal and home life, I could be quite irresponsible.

Take note of some ways that you may be contradictory in your life as well. When I started to dissect this about myself, I could see that I felt pressure to be responsible at work because I learned in my childhood that I had to be independent and take care of myself. In my personal life however, I sometimes found myself being the complete opposite. I just wanted to let go and play, and be the carefree little girl that didn't have to be so responsible. This was my shadow aspect finding ways to express itself. This behavior also got me in trouble at times, and made my life a mess! This is what happens when you strongly identify with your persona for most of your life. If we identify very strongly with our persona, then we will have a denser shadow. After shadow integration, I have found other ways to have my inner child's needs met without being irresponsible! If we don't ever allow our shadow to have it's needs met because it is so deeply suppressed and we are too concerned with portraying our persona, then we can have a complete pendulum swing in the opposite direction. This is when it causes problems. This can also be the cause of the so called 'mid life crisis'. It is just our shadow screaming to come out and have it's needs met.

After reflecting on your previous answers, can you see how you stronly identify with your persona? Were you able to see areas in your life where you might find yourself being the opposite? Or even just wanting to if you don't feel comfortable acting on it?

_____

28) Now, write down three words that would describe the opposite of your positive qualities. (e.g. Independent, resilient, and considerate/sweet are my 3 qualities. The opposite of those qualities are irresponsible/dependent, weak/victim, inconsiderate /selfish.)

_____

_____

_____

29) Once you have listed your 3 opposite traits, describe how you feel when you see people embody those 'negative' traits (e.g. I am disgusted when people play the victim role.)

_____

_____

_____

30) Do you harshly judge others when they are embodying those traits that are the opposite of your positive or persona traits?

_____

31) With each opposite 'negative trait', think of a time that you learned from others or decided for yourself that it was bad to be that way. (e.g. I learned that I couldn't act like a victim because no one was going to save me. Saying 'poor me' only made me feel worse and nobody cared. This made me realize that being the victim was pathetic and served no purpose. Therefore, I am highly triggered when I see, what I consider to be, people playing 'the victim role'.)

(I will give you an example of this exercise on the following page.)

<u>Quality</u> and <u>it's</u> opposite:

- Resilient (opposite ~ weak/victim): These type of people are pathetic and expect things to be handed to them. They are a burden and.. No one likes their energy.

- Considerate & Sweet! (opposite ~Selfish/inconsiderate): no one likes selfish people. They hurt & take from you. They don't care about anyone but themselves.

- <u>Independent</u> (opposite ~ lazy/ loser): they can't take care of themselves. They are a burden. They are weak and have no will power and drive.

*(answer question #31 below)

_____

_____

_____

_____

_____

_____

_____

_____

"The persona is a complicated system of relations between individual consciousness and society, fittingly enough a kind of mask, designed on the one hand to make a definite impression upon others, and, on the other, to conceal the true nature of the individual."

CARL JUNG

Understanding Your Shadow

Those opposite qualities of your persona that you just listed, those are shadow aspects that live inside of you. So what does that mean for me? I literally detest when people play the victim. I am not a victim. How is that living in my shadow? Does that make it a part of me? So, you may be saying the same thing about those undesirable traits that you just wrote down. That is not who you are. You work very hard to make yourself the opposite of that. It is important to understand that the words that we used are just a small aspect or a flavor, we could say, of the quality that you have denied. This doesn't mean it's necessarily a quality that you truly posses that you have denied, (although it could be). It could also just be a characteristic that you were never allowed to embody because it was deemed undesirable... whether you denied it yourself or you were forced to by your parental figures, family, or society. So, to continue with my example of victim. I was never allowed to play the victim... so that is how it was denied in me. Thusly, I proudly created a persona that identified strongly with being resilient.

32) Now, I want you to pick one of your 3 undesirable words that you feel most triggered by and resistant to being. Write down how you deny it like I denied the victimhood, and ask yourself if were forced to deny it by your family or society? Take some time thinking about all 3 qualities and why you deny them.

_____

_____

_____

_____

_____

(*here is an example. You can see here that my shadow desires to be allowed to be the so called 'victim')

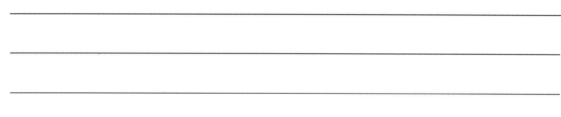

32) I am triggered by victim mentality because I had to deny ever playing the victim because no one cared and it just made me feel worse. I was told to suck it up. I wish I could've been allowed to ask for help and to feel sorry for myself more and receive more compassion for my struggles and hard work.

I'd like to give you another example on the following page in case you are having a hard time connecting with your undesirable shadow traits. If you remember one of my other traits that is an aspect of my persona is that I identify as sweet/considerate. The opposite of sweet/considerate is inconsiderate/selfish. I consider that to be rude! I don't relate to wanting to be rude at all! I mean, I can relate a little to wishing I could've played the victim at times in my life... but being rude or selfish? No way! I mean, no one likes inconsiderate, rude or selfish people! I'd like to add, that it's important to understand that we can acknowledge other peoples negative traits, but not be so strongly triggered by them. Whereas, I couldn't stand selfish or inconsiderate people, my friend might just brush it off as 'whatever, that's just how they are.'

There is a subtle difference when we are strongly triggered by certain things as opposed to just acknowledging others' negative traits. Let's start to dig a little deeper into the adjectives inconsiderate and selfish.

So, now let's look at some reasons I view inconsiderate/selfish as bad, and why I might try extra hard to be super sweet:

- Inconsiderate/selfish people don't think about others needs. they always put them selves first. They hurt and walk all over people.
- Inconsiderate/Selfish people probably have no friends and don't have many deep connections.
- Inconsiderate/Selfish people will receive bad karma and be punished.
- Inconsiderate/Selfish people are not liked by others and are probably lonely.
- Inconsiderate/Selfish people are empty inside and lack love since they only care about themselves.

Now, I can see that I clearly have no shadow desire to be selfish, but when I look at this list, I can see why I would completely avoid it. It means that I would have no love in my life. Love was the thing I was most desperate for, and losing people was my biggest fear.

Ok, so stick with me on this one, because I'm going somewhere here! Now let's take a look at the list of bad reasons to be selfish and inconsiderate. Obviously no one likes selfish people! This is just to show you why I would overcompensate by being extra sugary sweet... at times to a fault. This is also why I get extra triggered when I feel someone is rude by being inconsiderate or selfish. Because I never got to be selfish. Whereas, some people might just brush off somewhat rude, it infuriated me. The reality is that I would subconsciously think it's not fair that I have to people please and self sacrifice to get love and attention. Why do they get to just do and say what they want, and people still love them? This is what we mean by shadow. My strong reaction to that behavior was my shadow aspect projecting its desire to be loved without having to self sacrifice and be sweet all the time. Understanding this helps me to not overreact when I am triggered by this behavior. Once I can see that shadow aspect of myself, I can observe ways that I may be portraying my sweet/considerate persona to a fault causing me to self sacrifice at times. Aside from understanding why I identify so strongly with being kind, to the point where I self sacrifice, this also helps me to understand that there is an aspect of me that I repressed in my shadow that never got to be selfish. Which is really at the core of what I am associating rude with. So, now I can ask myself... what are some good things about being a little selfish? What would happen if I let myself take a small little homeopathic dose of being selfish? Maybe I would choose myself and not stay in unhealthy relationships, or maybe I would be better at setting boundaries at work, or not people please and self sacrifice so much. I would probably feel less resentful when I see people being able to set clear boundaries.

33) Of your 3 opposite traits, what is the trait that you find yourself being most resistant to?

_____

34) Now do the same as I did for the word inconsiderate/selfish, and write down all the reasons it's bad to be that way.

_____

_____

_____

_____

_____

35) Make a list of what would happen to someone who never stopped being that way?

_____

_____

_____

_____

_____

36) What do you fear experiencing the most on that list if you were to embody that trait? (For example: in my case, it would be not being liked by others or having no real connections in my life. That is why I believed I had to earn love by being sugary sweet. Otherwise, I would end up alone and without love. (I also don't want to hurt people, but hurting people also means that you can lose them.) This is where we discover the fear behind rejecting the trait.

_____

_____

_____

_____

_____

_____

To give you a better understanding of why this is such a huge fear for me... I had a very lonely childhood. I grew up as an only child, and I was always home alone I couldn't play outside when my mom and step dad were gone. I was desperate for company and connection. Therefore, I learned that if I was always a super sweet nice girl, that I would be liked and have connections. Hence my kind persona. This has actually been detrimental in my life causing me to self sacrifice, people please, have poor boundaries, and accept poor behaviors from my romantic partners. Contemplate this idea for a moment of over compensating just to have your needs met. Maybe if my childhood wasn't so lonely, I wouldn't have those subconscious needs. I could choose myself and wouldn't see that as selfish. Knowing that now, I can find ways to nurture my own inner child without needing to self sacrifice.

37) Does the good quality that you created as part of your persona serve a purpose to allow you to get your needs met in some way? If so, in what way? (for example: my being sweet got me love and connection).

_____

_____

38) Ask yourself if you can find a way to see anything good about being those so called negative traits that you listed as the opposite of your traits you are proud of.

_____

_____

_____

You can somewhat adjust the word as well if you need to just to not feel so aversed to that word. I associated the word inconsiderate with selfish. By asking myself what good could come of me being selfish, I could look at it as a way of choosing myself instead of people pleasing. If I didn't always just be super sweet to people even when they disrespected me, I would be more respected and stand up for myself. You can see how being able to embody these things on a smaller scale would be a good thing. To integrate that shadow aspect inside of me that desires to be loved without having to self sacrifice, I could do little things every day to choose myself. I could set more boundaries and not people please so much. I could say NO more and see that people still love me for who I am. I might even gain respect, and, in turn, respect myself more. How does this show up for you?

It's also important to understand that we may risk losing people as well when we start to choose ourself first. Unfortunately, this can reinforce our shadows reason for suppressing those things in the first place. When we stay strong and continue to choose ourselves, we risk losing loved ones. That is a risk you have to be willing to take if you are on a path of true personal development. When I started choosing myself more, I lost people that I was closest to, and it was truly heartbreaking. I can say now, with absolute certainty, that I am much happier now. I used to admit fault when I shouldn't have just to stay connected. I gave my time and energy when I had none to give to myself just to make others happy. I even drank, ate unhealthy, and partied with friends when I didn't want to just to feel a sense of commaraderie and closeness. These relationships were built on this dynamic of me self sacrificing, so naturally they would fall away when I decided to choose myself. We also have to acknowledge our responsibility in practicing this behavior and avoid placing blame on others. This is difficult, but I promise you that when you heal that shadow aspect, you open up room in your life for healthier relationships. You give your subconscious mind the green light to start attracting better people and things in your life since you no longer need to heal that shadow aspect.

At this point now, you should have a greater understanding of why our shadow aspects are typically the opposite of our persona. Now that you can have a little compassion for why your shadow might desire a tiny dose of those so called negative traits like selfish or victim, you can begin to start to integrate and accept those aspects of yourself. Once we begin to integrate those shadow aspects, we will no longer attract in those relationships that can turn toxic becuaese we are trying to have our shadow's needs met through them.

That is when we attract the friendships and relationships that are healthy, and it's not necessary to try to manipulate them into healing our inner child's wounds.

39) Now, make a list of why would it be good to take a tiny little homeopathic dose of one of your negative traits. Take note of all the ways that your life could improve if you allowed yourself to allow that trait in more.

_____

_____

_____

_____

_____

_____

In case you're having a hard time connecting with your negative trait, below is an example. I gave the example of selfish before, but to give you some further understanding, I will use the example of my victim shadow aspect. Here are a few things that would happen if I would take a smaill homeoptathic dose of 'victimhood':

- I would feel more comfortable asking for help
- I wouldn't be so stressed and tired if I could ask for help and be comfortable receiving it.
- I could share my feelings sadness and fears instead of denying my feelings, and then I could work on releasing my feelings instead of repressing them.
- I would feel like people understand my struggles a little bit more and that would feel good. I would feel more understood and validated.
- I would feel less resentful about all my responsibilities and probably feel happier.
- This might open my life up to more play with loved ones and a deeper connection.

So, you can see that my victim aversion, is just my shadow's desire to be worthy to receive, and seek compassion and understanding. Allowing some of this in my life could be so healing on many levels. My being turned off by seeing others feel worthy of seeking compassion, was just a projection of my deep subconscious feelings of unworthiness. Realizing this now, I can have the conscious awareness to know that I am inherently worthy of receiving and asking for help. To heal this shadow aspect, I could take small steps everyday to get more comfortable with that. How does this translate in your case?

Shadow Projections

We've all said it before... "oh jeez, she's just projecting!" Or, "stop projecting your own insecurities onto me!" Ouch... that just sounds so harsh and negative, doesn't it? The truth is, we all project... all day every day. It's impossible not to. Projections are images we have of others which are generated by the psyche and based in our own fears, desires, impulses, and unresolved issues. Most of which are unconscious. We see others not as they are, but as we are... that is why we call it mirroring. As humans living our own subjective experience, it's impossible to see the world objectively. Everything we do in life is colored through the lens of our personal past experiences, our past traumas, and past conditioning. When we choose a movie, we are projecting our judgements about how good it might be based on our past cinematic experiences. It's just that simple. So get comfortable with the word 'projection,' Your ego won't like it, but the sooner you accept the fact that you're projecting your own judgements onto the world ALL the time, the sooner you can open your eyes and see how your judgements about other people show you what you need to heal! The antidote to projection is authenticity. When we are authentic about who we truly are, shadow and all, we also become more able to see others for who they truly are. Only then can you become a master of transcending your ego and taking accountability. This will make you unstoppable! You will not feel so triggered, and all your relationships will improve.

When we can transcend our ego, take accountability and admit that our judgements of other people show us what we need to integrate, we can transmute our fear into courage. Our pain becomes a catalyst for strength and resilience, and suppressed anger can be brought into the light to be transmuted into warrior like passion! So, just accept the fact that the darkness you see in other people lives inside of you too. Only then, can you bring it into the light to be transmuted into your superpower!

"Projections change to world into a replica of one's own face."

CARL JUNG

Bringing Light Into the Dark

Do you see how I was able to dig deep to search for the 'light' aspects of victimhood? Really it just translated as feeling worthy of asking for help and comfort, which I didn't feel growing up. I knew that my parents loved me, but I didn't want to inconvenience them with my needs, and I learned to continue that into adulthood. That is why I got so triggered when I see other people feeling sorry for themselves or asking for help all the time. I was just projecting my unlived and unmet needs onto them, and shaming them for being so-called 'victims' when often times, it's just people that feel comfortable asking for help, expressing their needs, and feeling worthy to share their hardships. The same goes for rude or selfish people. If I would allow myslef to take a homeopathic dose of selfish, I would have much better boundaries.

40) Now that you have made your list, Were you able to see any benefit of taking that tiny little 'homeopathic' dose of your so called negative trait? What did you learn?

_____

_____

_____

_____

41) How can you see that you may be projecting when you get triggered by people embodying that trait?

_____

_____

_____

42) Think of a person in your life that triggers you and embodies that negative trait. Do you think that you may have felt triggered by them so much because of your own projections? If so, can you have more compassion for them now?

_____

_____

_____

_____

Throughout your daily life, try to find little ways to express your shadow and have it's needs met. This is where the true shadow work happens and how we begin to heal and integrate our shadow. Now that I have become comfortable with acknowledging that there is an aspect inside of me that craved feeling worthy of being the victim, I can work on healing that. That would look like asking people for help, being vulnerable and sharing when I am feeling overwhelmed by life, knowing that I am worthy of having needs and receiving from people. To heal and integrate the shadow aspect that decided that choosing myself was bad or selfish, and that I always had to be extra nice to feel loved, I could do things like stop self sacrificing, or leave unhealthy relationships, and speak up for myself more. You see where I am going with this?

Take some time to write down some pratical things you could do daily to integrate that so called undesirable shadow aspect and have it's needs met. Think of anything, big or small, that you could do to integrate that aspect of you or show it compassion. For example:

- To integrate my shadow aspects with my independent persona, I can allow myself to take a day off and ask someone for help. I could let my boyfriend pay for some things this month and know that I am not a burden.
- To integrate my shadow aspects with my resilient persona, I can allow myself to talk about my hardships and seek comfort and compassion. I could allow myself to cry when I need to instead of holding it in..
- To integrate my shadow aspects with my considerate/sweet persona, I could set stronger boundaries in relationships, and choose myslef first in my life instead of self sacrifice.

You can use the previous series of questions (#41-42) anytime when you find yourself becoming extremely triggered by someone's personality, and placing judgements on them. That is usually an indicator that the thing that you are triggered by is usually what is in your shadow. This is why we call it projection. For example, when I am triggered by seeing the victim mentality, I am just projecting my desire to allow that for myself. Seeing what triggers you in other people is a great way to uncover more of your shadow aspects. I'd like to add that our shadow may also be triggered by so called positive qualities you see in other people that you may deem annoying (aka: being triggered by the 'Golden Shadow'.) This is when we find ways to make someones positive attributes negative and judge them for it. This is usually because we have subconsciously denied ourselves from embodying those traits or we weren't allowed to by our parental figures or society. Below is an example so you can get a better understanding:

So, I used to get super annoyed when I would see certain people be overly confident. I would judge the ways that they were seemingly over inflating their talents. I would find myself thinking... 'Who do they think they are? Oh, they're in for a rude awakening when they fail... they shouldn't be so arrogant. Don't they know you shouldn't count your eggs before they're hatched?!' Now, knowing that my triggers point directly to my shadow, I can look at why their confidence would annoy me so much. I should be happy for them that they are so confident, but my shadow is only projecting it's own desire to be confident onto them. I was triggered by their confidence, and we already know that the shadow can get triggered by its opposite. That probably means that somewhere deep in my subconscious, I am insecure and I wish to be confident. So, now I can see that my shadow desires confidence, and I can see that I judge what I consider to be too much confidence, as a negative trait in other people. I view it as arrogant. Even though i desire confidence, I can still see it as negative or arrogance in other people. This is what we call projection. Get it??!

By just observing what triggers me in other people, I can have a better understanding of how I might acutally be yearning to be like them on a subconscious level. The realization of this immediately checks me from judging them and allows me to turn my judgements about them into a goal to strive towards. This subtle shift in attitude is shadow integration.

"Nothing has a more divisive and alienating effect upon society than this moral complacency and lack of responsibility, and nothing promotes understanding and rapprochement more that the mutual withdrawal of projections."

CARL JUNG

Golden Shadow

Now that we've touched on our 'darker' shadow aspects, let's explore how you may have a well of untapped potential locked away and hidden in your shadow. This is what we call our 'Golden Shadow.' Some reasons that we may have supressed talents, hobbies, or hidden potential into our shadow could be fear of judgement, shame, or fear of making other people feel bad in comparison. Let's take the example I gave in the masterclass of Tommy who loved to dance as a boy. He was an amazing dancer with unbelievable flexibility. He picked up choreography faster than anyone. It was his passion, but when he reached 6th grade, the boys in school bullied him and called him girly and gay. He was bullied so bad that he quit and never looked back. He denied ever even wanting to dance. He put all of his energy into intellectual pursuits, and even forgot how to dance. Now, as an adult, he hates weddings or events where there is dancing. He judges every male dancer as girly, but he feels a void inside of him that he can't explain. Another example could be caused by a sibling dynamic where 2 sisters both love to sing and act. Let's say the little sister Jenny idolized her older sister and she would do anything to spend time with her. This included practicing her lines for the school play. She learned to love acting as well, and it was something fun they could do together. Eventually, Jenny started getting all the leading roles because she was a better natural actress. This caused her older sister to feel bad and stopped spending time with her. Jenny was so devastated about losing her sister's affection, whom she idolized, that she decided to quit acting.

She said it took up too much of her time and she didn't like it anymore. After that, her sister came back around and they were close again. Can you see how Jenny's desire to feel close with her sister would cause her to tell herself she doesn't like acting anymore? She grew up believing it. Now, as an adult, she sees acting as a waste of time and always finds an excuse to skip her sister's plays. Jenny also learned on subconcious level that if she shined too bright that she would lose the people that she loved. This caused her to continually diminish her talents in all areas of her life. She stayed small and always remained the underdog despite her vast array of talents, because she didn't want to make other people feel bad and lose relationships. Now that she is approaching mid life, she feels a deep sense of failure and sadness, and doesn't understand why. So, based on these two examples, you can see how our desperate need for love and acceptance as children could cause us to completely deny even amazing talents. So much so, that we don't even relate to that talent anymore. However, we might catch ourselves being moved by seeing someone express that talent or even feel triggered and annoyed, and call them a show off. Our reaction to the golden shadow can manifest in many different ways. It's so important to see what is hidden in the golden shadow if we want to live a fully authentic life.

Those untapped potentials or hidden desires can hold the key to discovering our souls higher calling. It's so much more than discovering latent talents, it's becoming aquainted to a part of your beautiful self that you once loved that has been denied. It's coming into union with all parts of yourself so you can realize your place in the world and serve your soul's higher purpose. So, let's explore what latent hidden talents might be under the surface of your shadow waiting to see the light of day!

43) What are some conscious talents that you have that you are proud of?

_____

_____

_____

44) Do you truly enjoy doing those things now?

_____

_____

45) Are they talents that your parental figures encouraged you to foster in childhood that you just continued into your adult life?

_____

_____

_____

46) Was there any extracurricular activities you felt pressure to participate in growing up? If so, what were they?

_____

_____

47) If so, what would you rather have been doing?

_____

_____

48) What made you feel alive as a child?

_____

_____

_____

49) What were your daydreams about? Do you still have those daydreams?

_____

_____

_____

50) What were your hobbies and interests as a child? Did you stop any of those and why?

_____

_____

_____

51) When you were a kid, what did you want to be when you grew up?

_____

_____

52) Did you think that it was possible to be that?

_____

53) Did anyone tell you that it was silly or not possible to be that thing? Explain. (if so, take this memory to the Inner Child Reflections Meditation)

_____

_____

54) Did your parental figures encourage you to pursue the things that you enjoy or did they put pressure on you to do what they thought you should do?

_____

_____

55) Did you ever have a talent or interests that you were too shy to show or explore? If so, why?

_____

_____

56) Were you ever made fun of for something that you loved growing up? Explain. (if so, take that memory to the Inner Child Reflections Meditation.)

_____

_____

57) If so, how did it make you feel, and did it cause you to quit?

_____

_____

58) As a child, did you ever feel guilt for shining bright or showing off?

_____

59) If so, who drove you to feel guilty and why? (If there were any people that called you a show off or told you to stay humble or adult figures that allowed others to say that to you, take that memory to the Inner Child Reflections Meditation.)

_____

_____

60) When you were a kid, were you ok with being different, or was fitting in more important to you? What about now as an adult?

_____

_____

61) Dig deep and honestly ask yourself who you feel envious of and why or if you can't think of anyone specific, what type of person are you envious of, or who do you admire and why?

_____

_____

62) Does that person make you feel inferior or insecure?

_____

_____

63) What quality of theirs would you like to embody?

_____

_____

64) Who did you idolize growing up and why?

_____

_____

65) Is there anyone you idolize or deeply admire as an adult and why?

_____

_____

66) If so, do you believe that it is possible to be like them? Why/not?

_____

_____

67) Are they anything like you in character or personality or could they be the complete opposite? (If they are opposite, their persona could be a golden shadow aspect in you. Explore that.)

_____

_____

68) Do you ever find yourself being pulled toward creative pursuits or new hobbies, but you don't know why or how to start?

_____

_____

69) If so, do you feel like it's too late to explore these new things or are you open to pursue them?

_____

70) Does a fear of starting something new and failing at it ever hold you back from trying those things that light you up? Explain.

_____

_____

71) Do you ever feel like something is missing in your life but you can't understand why? If so, explain.

_____

_____

72) Is there anything that you enjoy doing that you keep hidden because some people might think it's weird? (for example: hide your facination with the occult or do you hide your brainy side?)

_____

73) How can you find a community of like minded people who share those same interests?

_____

74) How do you make time for play & creative expression in your life?

_____

_____

75) Make a list of things that light you up as an adult and as a child.

_____

_____

76) What are some things you can do every day to have that need met to experience that thing?

_____

_____

77) What is something that you can do to try something new and get outside your comfort zone?

_____

_____

78) How can you get comfortable trying new things and failing?

_____

_____

After answering these prompts, did you discover any golden qualities you supressed into your shadow? If so, take some time to write a release letter to your younger self and aplogize to it for denying it's gifts. Make a promise to your younger self that you will take action to enjoy those gifts going forward. If your suppressed hidden talents or interests were denied due to bullying, guilting, or shaming, you can take that memory to the Inner Child Reflections Mediation. When you feel the letter is complete, burn the letter and set the ashes free.

Envy & the Shadow

Now that we understand that the Golden Shadow can be revealed to us through envy and admiration, let's segway into that big and bad topic of envy and how we judge others. Let's do a little deeper personal exploration to uncover how the things that we envy in other people can point to our shadow. Envy can be a difficult word to identify with because it has such a negative connotation. However, if we can just see envy as a desire to have, be, or do something that we see in other people, but we don't believe we can, we can see that envy is just a reasonable human emotion that everyone has on occasion. I'd like to acknowledge the difference between envy, admiration, and jealousy. Envy is a mix of admiration, desire, and a belief that we can't have, do, or be that thing. That can make us feel bad about ourselves or just cause us to feel extreme reverence for another. Admiration is when we feel good for other people and are happy for them. We can also envy and admire at the same time. For example: I really envy your attention to detail. I am not that patient! There is a sense of admiration there and a desire to be patient without showing contempt for the other person. However, jealousy is a little different, and can have a more petty connotation, in my opinion. Jealousy often has to do with a third party or something beyond our control. Or, it's our ego's need to possess someone or something or compete in some way. If we can find a way to turn jealousy or envy into admiration, that makes the thing that you are admiring or desiring possible for you to achieve. It makes it a potential goal to strive for. If you can admire it in someone else, then it must live inside of you somewhere! Whereas, jealousy just makes us feel as if it is not possible to ever have that thing that we envy or is a feeling of fear that we might lose something that we are insecure about being able to keep. For example: the older model was jealous of the younger model's youthful looks vs the older model envied her youth. There is a slight difference. The older model can still envy her youth without feeling jealous. Hopefully, this can get you more comfortable with using the word envy!

Take some time to answer the journal prompts on the next pages and really contemplate your answers to see what you can learn about yourself, and remember to be honest... this is for you and only you!

79) What are some things that you envy about other people?

_____

_____

_____

80) Do you believe that you are worthy or deserving of what they have?

_____

81) If the answer is yes, do you believe that you could ever have or be the thing that you are envious about?

_____

_____

82) If so, how are you taking steps towards accomplishing that?

_____

_____

_____

83) If you're not doing anything to attain it, what is holding you back?

_____

_____

_____

84) What is within your control that you can do to attain that thing?

_____

_____

_____

85) If this thing that you envy is completely out of your control or realm of possibility (such as looks, ethnicity, health, or age), how can you you find a way to accept that or do you feel frustration, anger, or sadness about it?

_____

_____

_____

When we have accepted the fact that it is out of the realm of possibility for us to be that thing, then we can transmute jealousy or envy into admiration. That is when you can be completely happy for that person that has those things as opposed to jealous. Can you see how accepting and admiring can be so freeing? This also raises our vibration and allows us to attract other positive things into our life that are unique to us.

86) What are some ways that you can transmute jealousy into admiration in your life?

_____

_____

87) If you answered no that you don't believe that you deserve the thing that you envy, then why do you think that is?

_____

_____

_____

88) Do you ever find yourself resenting or blaming your parental figures or other people for being the reason you can't be, have, or do something? If so, why and how can you take responsibility now?

_____

_____

_____

89) If not, Is it in your power to attain that thing? do you blame, shame or beat yourself up for not having it? Explain.

---

90) Was there a time in your early life when you tried to attain or do something, but the outside world doubted your ability or caused you to feel shame or guilt for wanting it? (for example: I wanted a cool new shoes like my friend when I was in junior high. I asked and my parents, but they told me we couldn't afford it. I saw that made my mom sad, so I felt guilt for asking.)

Can you see how that last example could cause me to feel guilt and even feel shame for being vain and wanting fancy things? This creates a shadow aspect of desiring nice things. Which can cause me to feel jealous or judge people that wear labels as vain or materialistic. It can also make a 12 year old believe that they aren't worthy of nice things, which can subconsciously cause me to block my ability to attain and attract nice things.

If you had any experience where something that you desired caused you to feel guilt or shame for wanting it, take that to the Inner Child Reflections Meditation to heal that. This will allow your to be more of a magnet to attract that thing that you desire.

91) Do you ever find yourself envying people's accomplishments or talents? Was there ever a time when you tried and failed at that thing you are envious about? How did that make you feel?

_____

_____

92) Do you ever feel resentment towards those people that can have or do those things that you can't?

_____

93) Did people ever make fun of you or make you feel bad for trying and failing? If so, take that memory to the Inner Child Reflections Meditation.

_____

_____

94) Do you believe it's possible to try again and achieve it?

_____

95) If so, how can you make steps towards doing that?

_____

_____

96) If not, how can you find ways to accept that and refocus that energy into something else?

_____

_____

97) Have other people's previous or potential judgements caused to you stay small and believe that you shouldn't or can't do that thing? How?

_____

_____

_____

Now let's talk about our judgements of other people. Do certain people ever really just get under your skin? Like the sight of their stupid face makes you just want to punch it, but you can't explain why?! Do you ever find yourself saying something like 'oh jeez... here comes Becky again acting so happy and fake all the time!'?

In the next exercise, we will dig a little deeper to understand why some people's personality might irk you to the point of wanting to react or feel distain, even if it's not justified. On the following pages, I have created a list of aspects that our shadow may be triggered by, and what the underlined projection or cause might be. This list contains only a small amount of endless triggering traits, but it is just to show you how we can distort others behaviors to suite our shadow's projections. This can cause us to judge, when in actuality, it may be from a place of envy or desire to allow ourselves to be that way. Keep in mind, this is for traits that you are specifically triggered intensely by, and cause you to judge other people harshly.

Triggering Traits

- inconsiderate - you could judge someone as inconsiderate if you were an after thought in your home growing up and now you over accommodate and call it considerate.
- outspoken - you could judge outspoken people if you were never allow to speak up as a child and were often scolded for talking.
- entitled - if you judge someone as entitled maybe you are resentful they get what they want and they believe that they are deserving and you never got what you wanted or have felt deserving
- victim - if you judge someone as the victim, maybe you never got to be shown compassion or allowed to feel sorry for yourself growing up. This could asp be a tiggering if you struggle with feelings of worthiness.
- needy - if you judge as needy, maybe you were never allowed to express your needs and you felt like a burden.
- fake/phony - maybe you judge their happiness as fake because you were never allowed to be excited about much growing up because you had a depressed parent or caretaker. Or, maybe someone in your childhood home made fun of you for celebrating or expressing joy.
- vain/extravagant - you could judge someone as vain or extravagant because maybe you never had nice things growing up or never felt beautiful. You could've also had a parent that said things like "money is the root of all evil."
- selfish - you could judge someone as selfish because you never got to choose yourself and now you self sacrifice
- perfectionist/picky - you could judge someone as a perfectionist if you lack control or lack follow through

- workaholic – you could judge hard work as being a workaholic because it triggers your lack of work ethic or maybe you had parents that were always working and never around
- arrogant – you could judge confidence as arrogance because you are insecue and lack confidence.
- push overs – you could judge kindness as being a push over because your mom was a push over with your dad or because you had to be one to feel safe
- know it all – you could judge confidence in sharing wisdom as a know it all because you never had the confidence to share your knowledge or maybe a parental figure always told you that you were wrong.
- show off – maybe you judge someone as a show off because you lack the confidence and pride in your self to share your gifts.

98) Now, identify some 'negative' triggering triats either form that list or some from your own list that really trigger you about other people. There are endless things we can judge people for, those are just some examples.

_____

_____

99) Why do those traits bother you so much and who in your life displays them?

_____

_____

_____

_____

100) Now, we will reference journal prompts #39-42 again and relate those annoying qualities you judge to those same questions.

Here are journal prompts #39-42 for reference:

- Make a list of why would it be good to take a tiny little homeopathic dose of that 'negative' trait. Take note of all the ways that your life could improve if you allowed yourself to allow that trait in more.

_____

_____

_____

_____

- Now that you have made your list, Were you able to see any benefit of taking that tiny little 'homeopathic' dose of your so called negative trait? What did you learn? How can you see that you may be projecting when you get triggered by people embodying that trait?

- Think of a person in your life that triggers you and embodies that 'negative' trait. Do you think that you may have felt triggered by them so much because of your own projections? If so, can you have more compassion for them now?

These series of questions when asked can soften the intense aggitation we might feel towards certian people and can make our life just feel lighter. It can help us to see that the things that we often judge in other people come from our shadow's envy and desire to be allowed those things. Then we can take small steps every day to add that little 'homeopathic' dose of that thing that our shadow so desperately needs. We can alchemize and heal those parts of us by having compassion for other people and for our shadow. Once we are able to do that, we can discover what subconscious need our shadow is desperate to have met and find little ways to do that every day. Now, getting back to the example of annoying, fake Becky... can you allow yourself to have more appreciation for Becky's fake (aka cheerful) personality?! Can you see ways that you may actually be envious that other people can freely express these traits that you couldn't. That's when we label those traits as 'negative' when often times they are not. Can you acknowledge that somewhere deep on a subconsious level, your shadow may be yearning to express those things too? One could ask themselves if, at some point in their upbringing, were they not allowed to express joy or get too excited because of a depressed parent or an insecure sibling. Or, another cause with this example could be that their home was extremely depressing and they never felt joy, so they could end up subconsciously resenting happy people. I know it can be a tough pill to swallow to view ourselves as judgmental or subconsciously envious, but this kind of realization can literally be a game changer in all of our relationships! When we start to see what we envy, we can understand what we think we can't have or don't deserve. And when we understand where the feeling of 'it's not possible for me' comes from, then we can do our best to heal it. For example, I used to attribute my friends success to her being a 'workaholic', and I judged it as bad. Now, I can try to uncover why I might make the idea of success a bad thing on a subconscious level. I can ask myself.... Was there ever a time in my early life when I learned that being successful meant that I had to work really hard and it was a bad thing? When I really think about that question, I can recall that when I was a child, I was always alone because my Mom and my stepdad were always gone at work. I was raised as an only child, so I was very lonely growing up. My Mom and stepdad worked all hours of the day and night, but they were factory workers and didn't make much money. I remember growing up with a sense of feeling that you had to work hard to make money, because I saw how hard they worked. The same thing happened when I went to stay with my Dad. He was always working in the garage, and it took away from our time together. So, to me, on a deeper subconscious level, I only see success as hard work, and it takes you away from the people who love and need you. And, hard work to my inner child means that I am left all alone. It triggers my feeling of abandonment. So, I grew up wanting to have great success so that I wouldn't have to work so hard and be absent when I have a family... BUT, on a deeper subconscious level outside of my conscious awareness, I viewed success as hard work, which meant that it takes up all your time. No wonder why my subconscious mind would try to sabotage my dreams of being successful!

101) Was there ever a time in your early life that you learned that being that thing that you envy (that you judge) could be bad or cause you discomfort or suffering? (e.g. I envied success and good work ethic, but judged it as 'workaholic' because I learned as a child that hard work makes you abandon loved ones.)

_____

_____

_____

To give you another example, you could envy someone for their sexy figure and wish you could lose weight and look like them. But, maybe growing up, you had an overweight family member that tried to lose weight and was always complaining about how hard it is to diet and how miserable it is, and that It's better to be fat and happy! This can program your subconscious mind to relate skinny with miserable. Or, maybe you or someone in your life was sexually assulted, so on a subconscious level you believe that having a sexy figure means that you are in danger, causing your subconscious mind to keep weight on.

I know this might sound crazy to think that we are denying ourselves the things that we desire most, but that is just how sneaky our subconscious mind is when it is trying to protect us. It is operating on auto pilot without our knowledge. And, that is why envy hurts so bad, because we deeply desire that thing, but for some reason, seemingly beyond our control, we believe we can't have it. So, what's the point of exploring what we envy in other people?! Well, we know that what we envy points to our shadow. But, exploring even further, we can begin to see why we might feel that these things are so unattainable. And, when we can understand that it's just our subconscious mind limiting us out of our deeper fears, we can start to realize that what we envy in others is actually possible for us! That's when we can turn that envy into admiration and free ourselves! HALLELUJAH! Envy or Jealously is an extremely low vibrational feeling that will only bring in more things to be envious of and more lack into your life. But, the moment we can shift our perspective and realize that our deeper feelings of envy are just our shadow judging our potential to have something based on our subconscious fears, then we can strive to attain that thing! When we turn envy into admiration, we become a magnet to being admirable! It's so important to realize that if we can see something in someone else that we want, that the potential of it already lives inside of us, and is yearning to come out.

102) Can you see why your subconscious mind may be thwarting those things you desire that you envy in other people? (like my lack of success due to my subconscious mind fearing the work) Explain how this shows up in your life.

_____

_____

_____

Take a moment to write down the fear behind why your subconscious mind might deem it to be bad. For example:

My subconscious fears my being successful because that takes me away from my loved ones and means I have to work too hard. I subconsciously view success as causing stress. That could be why it causes me to be so perfectionistic and to procrastinate and sabotage my success!

_____

_____

_____

_____

Now I can understand why my sneaky, covert subconscious mind might be sabotaging my success! I can have a conscious awareness now and bypass those perfectionistic or procrastinating moments with a greater understanding and forge ahead to accomplish my goals!

103) Knowing that now, do those things feel any more attainable to you?

_____

_____

104) What is one thing that you can do now to work towards attaining it?

_____

_____

_____

105) Are you comfortable or ok with not attaining it? If not, why?

_____

_____

106) Do you believe that the good AND the bad that you see in other people is a reflection of what is in you?

_____

_____

107) Can you realize that what you judge is a shadow aspect of you? How can you learn to have compassion for others when you find yourself judging their flaws?

_____

_____

_____

Be Real, but Kind to Yourself

This kind of digging deep and self awareness requires a level of honesty about yourself that can be extremely difficult. In the past that would have felt shameful for me to even admit in this workbook that I judged someone's confidence or that I desire to be worthy of playing victim. But, I have done enough shadow integration to be ok with it, and I have found ways to become more confident and integrate my insecure shadow that didn't feel good enough or worthy of sympathy. That's why they always say that shadow work is difficult. It requires a level of deep honestly with yourself. It calls for you to really let go of your ego's need to identify with the persona, and admit where you may have been an asshole! And once you identify that asshole, it's also important to love it and have compassion for it. Because you know what... That part of you that you deem undesirable, that I just called an asshole... that is just a part of you that is desperate to be healed. It's coming up to the surface to be soothed and loved. Most of the time, it is just your inner child yearning to be seen and healed and validated! It's your inner child screaming to get it's needs met, so it's important to have love, compassion, and understanding for it. We have to find ways to meet those needs of our inner child ourselves. That shadow aspect of me had learned to be insecure because, as a child, my stepdad called me fat and made fun of me, so i grew up to be insecure and thought I could never do anything right. I learned to judge people that were confident as having an over inflated ego. When, really that's all I ever wanted to be. It was my inner child just wanting to heal and desiring what I denied. I'd like to note that we can develop our shadow traits at any age. However, most times, it happens in childhood when we are most vulnerable and desperate for acceptance. If, at any time you are feeling a need to make amends with your inner child and give it love or comfort, feel free to write a release letter and tell it everything you want it to know and wished it received when you were younger. You can make a promise to your inner child to always put it first and meet it's needs and let it know that it is safe now. After writing the letter, check in with your heart to feel if it is complete. And, always make sure to burn and release the letter when you are finished.

So, now we can see that our shadow can be triggered by seeing things in people that we don't ever want to be because we learned that it was bad (e.g. my victim aversion). AND, our shadow can also be triggered by things we wish we could be, but our ego has found a way to label those traits as bad (e.g. confidence is arongance.) When we understand that our shadow is usually born from a difficult time in our early life, we can start to see much quicker when our shadow was formed. Sometimes, just having the awareness of that shadow aspect and how it became suppressed, is enough to heal it. Just remember to consciously do things every day that contribute to the integration of those shadow aspects. We aren't getting rid of those things things, we are just finding ways to meet the needs of those shadow aspects. When we consistently do that, we become less reactionary when our shadow gets triggered. Being triggered might not ever end, but with shadow work, our strong desire to overreact will eventually dissipate.

"In every adult there lurks a child – an eternal child, something that is becoming, is never completed and calls for unceasing care, attention and education. That is the part of the human personality which waits to develop and become whole."

CARL JUNG

✦ What is Holding You Back? ✦

The next series of questions is to help you to discover what ways your shadow aspects have been holding you back from creating your dream life. Now, remember what we learned from the Shadow work presentation about our subconscious mind... it's main concern is just keeping you safe and alive. Sometimes that could look like finding ways to make you self sabotage your own life and your plans. All in the name of protecting you from something that it doesn't want you to experience. Do you ever find yourself engaging in behaviors that prevent you from making progess, but you just can't seem to stop? That could be anything from laziness, to perfectionism to self criticism and self doubts. There are endless ways that we can hinder our own progress. The irony is, we are holding ourselves back and don't even realize it! You see, your subconscious mind is causing you to embody this trait or behavior that you dislike so much for a reason. Otherwise, it wouldn't be such an issue for you to stop indulging in. So, let's dig a little deeper to find out why we might be sabotaging our own dreams!

108) What is the one behavior that you do or characteristic that you embody that you highly dislike about yourself? List Something that you feel tends to hinder your life in some way or something that causes you to self sabotage.

_____

_____

109) Once you have discovered your quality that you dislike, look for ways that your subconscious mind might actually WANT you to behave this way. What would be one benefit of you continuing this behavior? Is it protecting you in some way? Explain.

_____

_____

_____

_____

110) How is your subconscious protecting you by causing you to be _____? (name that negative trait) Really dig deep on this one and think about how it might be beneficial for your subconscious mind on a larger scale unbeknownst to you.

_____

_____

_____

_____

I'll give you a personal example in case you're having a hard time with this one. My biggest downfall is my procrastination. I have all these great ideas and big plans and goals, and somehow I manage to procrastinate my life away! I will literally find a million other things to do that are semi-related to my goal... including just reading and learning about that thing instead of actually just doing the thing! I do this so I still feel somewhat productive, but when I reflect on my day, I can see that I have accomplished nothing of any real value. I just busied myself into thinking that I was productive. Then I always think to myself, 'I'll get it all done tomorrow'... but tomorrow is just the same. This is so annoying because it is so covert when it happens, and I can't get mad at anyone but myself. It causes me to question my passions and fear that I don't even know what I want anymore. Queue the guilt and shame spiral into depression and self loathing! Ok, that's a tad dramatic, but at times it can be so disheartening and cause me to want to just give up on my big goals and dreams!

So, why would my subconscious actually cause me to procrastinate? What would the benefit be and how is procrastination keeping me safe? Well, If you're like me, then you're a dreamer and you have big, lofty goals and dreams of having, being, and doing it all. Having those kind of big dreams can cause you to fantasize and daydream and then you put a whole lot of damn pressure on yourself to accomplish them. The thought of not accomplishing them feels utterly devastating and like it's not even an option. Can you imagine what would happen if I actually did all those things that I was procrastinating on and then I actually failed? That would be heartbreaking. So... what if all that procrastination was my subconscious mind just sabotaging my plans because of my deep inner fear of failure?! I guess that would be one way that it could be protecting me, right?! If I busy myself with tasks that have to do with my goal, but not actually taking risks to do big things, then I will never fail, but I will think I'm being productive on a conscious level. This is how people waste years of their life and eventually end up quitting and disenchanted by their 'pie in the sky dreams'!

"Sometimes we self-sabotage just when things seem to be going smoothly. Perhaps this is a way to express a fear about whether it is okay for us to have a better life. We are bound to feel anxious as we leave behind old notions of our unworthiness. The challenge is not to be fearless, but to develop strategies of acknowledging our fears and finding out how we can allay them.

MAUREEN BRADY

So, now that you've discovered your so called 'toxic trait', can you see how it might be protecting you?

111) What is the fear behind the reason for your subconscious mind protecting you and sabotaging your life? (e.g. my fear was the fear of failure. The fear of not living up to my own expectations and then breaking my own damn heart with disappointment!)

_____

_____

So, now that we've discovered the fear, it's time to uncover where it came from.

112) Ask yourself... Why is it so bad to (name your fear) _____? (in my case it would be... Why is it so bad to fail and not accomplish my goal?) What would happen to you?

_____

_____

_____

113) Now once you have your answer... ask yourself... What would would I do? Could I handle it?

_____

_____

_____

114) What are some things within your power that you could do to make it better?

_____

_____

_____

115) Do you have any support system around you to count on if you experienced this fear? How would you rebound from this outcome if it happened?

_____

_____

_____

116) What are some things you could do daily to face this fear?

_____

_____

_____

The point of this is to get you to see that to face your fears and experience the worst case scenerio is never really as bad as we think it will be. We have just let our subconscious mind run the show forever, so we are paralyzed by it's fears and desire to keep us safe. And... the best way to stay safe is to play small. Those last series of questions can be a little confusing, but it's a game changer! So I've created a writing example on the next page to give you a better understanding of this.

Writing Example

What is one behavior that you do that holds you back?

One trait that holds me back in life is my perfectionism

What would be the benefit of this behavior?

My subconscious probably causes me to be this way because it keeps me in control of the outcome. I can make things perfect the way I like.

How is your subconsious protecting you by causing you to be this way?

It might be causing me to do this to protect me from failing because sometimes I never finish since It's not perfect. If I don't finish, I can't fail

What is the fear behind the reason for your subconscious mind protecting and sabotaging you?

The fear behind my perfectionism is probably the fear of failing or looking stupid or other people's judgements

Why is it so bad to be _A failure or be judged_ ?

It would be bad to fail at being perfect because people would judge me and I would feel humiliated. Everyone is expecting me to be perfect.

If this happened, what would you do? Could you handle it?

If this happened, I could handle it. I will just feel very shameful and humiliated.

What are some things you could do to make it better?

To make it better, I could just accept failure and try to start a new project and make that one a success.

How would you rebound from this outcome?

I could rebound from this outcome by getting back to work, putting less pressure on all my projects, and not caring so much about other people's opinions

What are some things you could do daily to face this fear?

Some things I could do daily to face this fear could be to be more flexible and practical with how I do things and how I present myself. I can stop caring so much about other peoples opinions. I could trust and release control and let other people do some of my work to be more efficient. I can see that people still see the value of what I do in other areas of my life without having to be so perfect. I can relax and take some pressure off of myself.

Fear is a Lie

Now, can you see how this bad habit or toxic trait you have is just your shadow's defense mechanism to protect you from being hurt and to get it's needs met? That is why it's so hard to conquer. Because our subconscious mind is literally running the show in our lives and we don't even realize it. We communicate with our subconscious mind through our feelings, and if the thought of failure, disappointment, or pain causes us to feel stress or sadness, then our subconscious will do whatever it takes to prevent that. That includes totally sabatoging our plans. Because It's only interest is keeping us safe. The point of that last exercise is to show that the root of our biggest fears is usually just potential failure and potential emotional suffering. We are sabotaging our dreams over a potential outcome that may or may not even happen! That means that many times we are denying our dreams and our highest timeline over a potentiality?! By looking at the worst possible outcome, we can see that the FEAR ITSELF of the suffering is worse than trying and failing and actually experiencing failure. WOAH! Can you believe that most of us have been unknowingly sabotaging our biggest goals over something that hasn't even happened?! And we don't even realize it! In turn, if we continue to chase our tail busying ourselves with with perfectionism (in my case), then we are failing anyway. So why not just go all in and fu@k#! fear?!

To allow you to dig a little deeper to understand how your shadow may be actually sabotaging your life, let's try another similar exercise. Below is a list of a few coping mechanisms that many people use to protect their shadow self or have it's needs met. See what behaviors that you can identify with and then answer the journal prompts on the following pages.

- perfectionism
- procrastination
- minimalising
- over analyzing
- over working
- over achieving
- people pleasing
- judging others
- blending in
- rationalizing
- distracting yourself
- anger/rage
- judging self
- avoidance
- laziness
- defensiveness
- yelling
- lying
- cheating
- over giving
- show off
- too outspoken
- too silenced
- no follow through
- unreliable

- clingy
- intelectualizing
- hyper sensitve
- self doubt/blame
- cutting/self mutilatin
- running away
- comparing
- addictions
- self sacrifice
- over worry
- over compensate
- mistrusting

Pick one of your main coping mechanisms from that list or a list of your own that your shadow uses to either protect itself or have it's needs met. We want to get aquainted with the idea that each of our shadow aspects has it's own autonomous personaility and set of needs. If we name it and treat it as a separate fragment, then it is easier for us to not make it so personal. Often times our coping mechanisms can be very toxic or damaging, so by treating it as a separate fragment that belongs to us, it prevents us from identifying with those behaviors so much. For example: if addiction is a coping mechanism, we could name it 'addict Joe', that gives more room for it to be an aspect of Joe that can be healed as opposed to Joe just identifying and claiming he IS an addict. This is helpful to do if you are doing shadow work by yourself and you don't have a coach to guide you. By doing this, we can bring it further to the light and give it the attention it needs. I will give some example answers for your understanding. I will use the coping mechanism of people pleasing.

So, I would start by naming this shadow aspect People Pleaser Sarah. I would ask it in this manner:

'So... People Pleaser Sarah...' (then ask)

117) What are you trying to protect me from?

I am trying to protect you from disappointing people and have my need met of feeling safe if I make people happy. I am protecting you from being alone. By pleasing others you make them happy and then they won't abandon you. Then you will be liked and people will need you.

118) Why would it be so bad for me to experience
<u>disappointing people and not making them happy</u> ?

If you disappoint people then they might think you don't have value and they might abandon you, and then you would end up alone.

119) At what age did you create this coping mechanism and why?

I created this coping mechanism when I was around 6 because my mom and step dad worked a lot and were always very stressed. I learned that if I was a good girl and did things to make them happy, then they wouldn't feel so overwhelmed and fight as much, and things would feel stable

120) What unmet needs are driving you to protect me?

My need to feel like my environment is safe, calm, and stable is driving me to protect you by people pleasing.

121) What emotion do you feel?

I feel anxious that I might lose people or be a burden.

122) What is something that I could do today to make you feel better and face this fear?

You could learn to say no more and start setting boundaries. You could choose yourself and the things that you like to do when you are making plans with people. You could allow yourself to receive instead of give. You could get comfortable being alone and plan a solo vacation. You could meditate for the anxiety or spend time in nature. You can practice a lot of self love to realize that you are lovable and you don't need to do anything to earn love.

If this shadow aspect of you (that is using coping mechanisms to stay safe) was created from an age in childhood and it was caused by any adults, I highly recommend using my inner child meditation with this exercise. This is one of the most powerful meditations I have, and my favorite way to do inner child work. Our shadow aspect is still at that same age that it experienced the initial trauma... that would be myself at 6 years old. Remember, our subconsios mind doesn't understand time. It only records experiences and feelings. This is why we call it inner child. Because it is still just a child and it needs to be healed from that time and place in your life. The Shadow Reflections Meditation is useful as well to explore a little further where your shadow aspect has come from, and it's not always necessarily from childhood. Also, take note of how your shadow aspect answers the last question #122. Do all those things as much as you can on a daily basis to meet that shadow aspect's needs. This is what we mean by shadow integration.

So, I will leave you with one last piece of advice on this topic of self sabatage and fear before we move on. I got this advice on a first date once from a super successful guy trying to give little ol' me some words of wisdom when I was uncertain about my life! It went something like this...

"When you're trying to decide if you should take a risk and you're scared to pull the trigger, just ask yourself these questions:

- If I took this risk and failed and lost it all, where would I be and could I survive it?
- If I could survive, what would I have to do, and what would it take to find my way out?
- Is this something that I could realistically find my way out of if I absolutely had to?

If you can answer yes to that question, you should always take the risk."

Although, I never had another date with that guy, that little golden nugget of wisdom has stuck with me! It's basically just stating that if you can look at that worst case scenario and find a way to solve that problem if it ever actually happened, then why the hell wouldn't you take a risk when it's something as huge as your biggest goals. and deepest desires and dreams? Because, in my humble opinion, trying, failing, and working like a dog to find your way out of a mess, is still better than never trying at all, and just wondering 'what if' for the rest of your life. You see, the most covert sabotage happens when we don't realize that we are being held back by fear. When we think we are doing something good on a conscious level by being a perfecionist or busying ourselves with menial tasks, we can waste our whole life away and chalk it up to 'oh well, I guess it wasn't meant for me.' Well, I'm here to tell you that that is absolutely absurd! If you can dream it up and desire it with all your heart, than it is meant for you. So go be fearless and take the damn risk!

"Do not be pushed around by the fears in your mind. Be lead by the dreams in your heart."

ROY T. BENNETT

Pride and Shame

So, as we learned earlier, we take pride in our persona, which points directly to what we feel shame about. Those are the things we supress into the shadow. Many people associate the word guilt with shame, but there are some differences. Guilt is feeling bad for something that you did or didn't do. Shame is believing that you are a bad person. There is a subtle difference. Guilt allows room for forgiveness and changed behavior, but shame is the inherent painful feeling of unworthiness. The truth is, everyone experiences shame to some degree. Deep shame is one of the lowest vibrational emotions that we can have, and when we are in shame, we can't be a vibrational match to our hearts true desires because that requires a feeling of worthiness. When shame is repressed deep into the shadows, we may not even know it's there, but we can feel a deep sense of unhappiness and unworthiness and not know why. This can cause us to attract many toxic relationships and circumstances. If we allow that shame to come to the surface, and we truly face it, we can begin to have more compassion for ourselves. By doing this, we can get closer to true self love and worthiness, which is what is needed to attract healthy relationships and to be a vibrational match to attract your hearts desires. Severe shame when repressed can cause us to react intensely or, in extreme cases, even violently, when we see that thing that we are ashamed of about ourselves in other people. A great exmple of this is extreme homophobia. Many homophobics are actually closeted homosexuals. If they grew up in a home or culture where it was completely unacceptable to be gay, then they will do everything in their power to repress those desires deep into their shadow. When they see open homosexuals freely and even proudly ebracing their homosexuality, that can trigger their deep shame and cause immense anger and rage. This is often where many acts of violence stem from. Take note of things that may trigger you in other people that cause almost a viceral negative reaction. Those could potentially be things you subconsciously feel shame for. Many times, we create a persona that is the opposite of the thing we are ashamed of. For example, the closeted homosexual becomes a pastor in a conservative church. Or maybe the little girl that had to repress her anger becuase she was taught that a proper girl does not show anger, grows up to become the docile compliant adult. But, she feels deep rage inside and gets very triggered when others are free to express their anger. As an adult, she may have outbursts of exrteme rage at times that she takes out on her children out of nowhere. This can, in turn, cause her to feel extreme shame causing her to repress that need to express her anger even deeper into the shadow. Identifying our shame can be very difficult for us because we've avoided it our whole lives. Some ways to identify shame are to paying attention to what you feel embarrassment   about, what you are keeping secret, where you blame other people when things go wrong, and what causes contmept within you when you spot that trait in other people.

Answer the journal prompts below to self reflect deeper on what you feel pride and shame for. These questions can bring up some heavy emotions, so be gentle with yourself, but brutally honest.

123) What are you most proud of about yourself and why?

_____

_____

_____

124) What achievement are you most proud of and why?

_____

_____

_____

125) What do you think other people are most proud of you for?

_____

_____

_____

126) Do you feel like you made your parental figures proud when you were growing up?

_____

127) Do you think you make them proud now if they are still alive? If they are not alive, do you think they would be proud of you?

_____

128) When do you feel you made them the most proud growing up?

_____

_____

129) Do you still try to do that thing to make people proud of you as an adult?

_____

130) Could this have been a factor in creating your persona?

_____

131) Do you feel shame if you don't make people proud? How important is it to you that you make your loved ones proud?

_____

132) Do you have any secrets that you would never want to share? If so, why?

_____

_____

133) Do you have a trusted friend, coach, or therapist you could share your deepest secrets with? If not, would you be open to reaching out to find one and sharing your secrets?

_____

134) What do you fear would happen if someone knew your deepest secrets?

_____

_____

135) What makes you feel shame and why?

_____

_____

_____

136) When you think of that thing, what emotion do you feel?

_____

137) Does that emotion feel unbearable to you or can you find a way to face it, feel it, and move through it?

_____

138) What is one thing you can do daily to conquer that thing?

_____

139) How can you find a way to have empathy and compassion for that part of you that you are ashamed of?

_____

_____

140) Do you ever find yourself judging other people for embodying that quality you feel shame for?

_____

141) When was the last time you felt shame and why?

_____

_____

_____

142) What are some things you do to cope with the emotion of shame or conquer that feeling?

_____

_____

143) Do you ever self medicate or battle addictions of any kind?

_____

144) If so, what do are avoiding feeling and why?

_____

_____

_____

145) Why would it be so bad to feel that feeing?

_____

_____

_____

146) What do you feel embarrassed about?

_____

_____

_____

147) Do you have an inherent sense of worthiness? Or, do you believe worthiness has to be earned?

_____

_____

148) If you answered no to that last question, ask yourself at what age did you decide this and why? If there was an adult that caused it during your childhood, take that to my Inner Child Reflections Meditation.

_____

149) Did you learn to feel shame for certain things growing up from either your parental figures or society? What for?

_____

150) Were you taught that is was bad to be or feel certain emotions? (If you answered yes, I highly recommend taking this topic to my inner child meditation and standing up for your younger self.)

_____

_____

151) What do you value most about people?

_____

_____

152) Did your parental figures express those values growing up? If not, what qualities did they express? How did that make you feel?

_____

_____

153) What were some negative traits about your parental figures growing up?

_____

_____

154) Do you embody these same traits or try to avoid them?

_____

155) Do you feel triggered when you see other people expressing their negative traits? If so, what emotions does this bring up in you. Explain. (Take that emotion to the Emotions Reflections Meditation to explore what you can learn there.)

_____

156) How do you handle or receive compliments, gifts, or favors?

_____

157) Do you feel like you have to immediately return compliments or favors? How can you feel more worthy of receiving without having to reciprocate?

_____

158) What happens when you make a mistake? Do you bounce back easily or feel bad about yourself and want to quit?

159) How can you find ways to keep trying and face potential failure?

160) Do you feel comfortable making eye contact with people? (especially when talking about uncomfortable things?) If not, this could point to shame. Can you work towards owning your story and confidently making eye contact?

161) How do you view vulnerability? (as a strength or a weakness? Why?)

162) Do you allow yourself to be vulnerable? If no, Why not?

163) How can you allow yourself to be more vulnerable?

_____

_____

_____

164) How do you handle criticism?

_____

165) Do you get overly defensive when you are criticized or accused of things?

_____

166) If so, were you often blamed or criticized as a child?

_____

167) If so, what age did you learn to become defensive and why? (If you answered yes, take this memory to the Inner child Reflections Meditation.)

_____

_____

_____

168) What do you think your inner child is protecting you from by being defensive now?

_____

_____

169) Ask your inner child what unmet need it has by being defensive (this could be something like 'I need to feel heard or safe) Then ask it 'What is one thing that I can do today to meet that need?'

_____

_____

_____

_____

If you are struggling with shame for anything in your life, take some time to write yourself a release letter. Set the intention to let go of all of these poisonous feelings. You can even speak to your shame and address it as it's own autonomous entity. Find what the feeling of shame is and use that to give it a name. If you feel shame because you experienced abuse, you can call it 'Victim Becky' or if you cheated, you can call it 'Cheater Bill.' You could say 'Thief Robin' or 'Loser Erin' or even just say 'Shameful Steve'. Let this part of you know that it is ok feel just, and offer it love and comfort. Let it know that you understand that it is sorry or that it feels unworthy or broken, but it is time let it go. Tell that aspect of you that this shame serves no purpose and you have a responsibiliy to let it go and even forgive yourself or others if you have to. Tell it all the ways that you will do better in its name and in its honor, so all of it's suffering is not in vain. Let the shame know that it can go now and vow to release it. Make sure to speak to that aspect of you with compassion, and let it know that it is inherently worthy of love, regardless of the past. As with all release letters, make sure to burn it and release the ashes.

As I stated earlier, if we don't address our shame and integrate those shadow aspects, we can battle a deep seated feeling of unworthiness and belonging for our entire lives. That can literally block us from abundance, healthy relationships, and true success. Here are a few things you can do to bring that shame into the light to heal it:

- Get comfortable expressing your needs and wants. This takes a level of worthiness in believing that we are deserving

- Receive compliments, favors, and gifts without feeling the need to reciprocate and just say thank you.

- Allow yourself to be more vulnerable and share your fears, feelings, and shame. This leads to authenticity which is the antidote to shame.

- When you notice any negative self talk or shame creeping in, imaging talking to yourself as you would a child.

- Take time to offer yourself love and compassion. That could look like taking a step back when the shame kicks in and just putting your hand on your heart and saying something like "I am ok. this feeling or thing doesn't define my worth." Imagine where shame would live inside your body and imagine yourself removing it and throwing it away!

- Get connected to your body through movement, grounding meditations, and breath work. Feel where the shame is in your body and send it love, shake it out, move it out of your body through visualization and movement.

- Many times we don't address our shame because we are running away from feeling an emotion. Go to my Emotion Reflections Meditation to learn from and move through that emotion. When examining your answers, if you are noticing that your shame was created in chilhood by certian adults or even society as a whole, take that to the Inner Child Reflections Meditation and stand up for that child.

- Find a friend, coach, or therapist that you are 100% comfortable with and share your deepest secrets that you feel shame about. It's important that this person is able to provide you with empathy.

- Once you have gotten comfortable being vulnerable or sharing your secrets, tell your story. Often times the thing that can be the most healing is when we have our pain and shame witnessed. It can give us a great sense of relief.

Often times shame can become our self concept if we were forced to be what our parents or society wanted us to be instead who we wanted to be. It sends the message that we can't be loved for who truly are. Speaking about our shame with people we trust allows us to face it and re-own it. When others offer our shame compassion and empathy, it gives us permission to as well. This helps us to integrate it allowing in more self love and feelings of worthiness.

"If we can share our story with someone who responds with empathy and understinding, shame can't survive in the light of empathy."

BRENÉ BROWN

The Shadow & Relationships

Now that we have a better understanding of how our shadow can cause us to judge, protect, and feel deep shame and envy, let's talk about my other favorite topic... the shadow and relationships! In the masterclass that I referenced in this workbook, we discuss the power of the subconscious mind and how it runs the show in our life. And if you recall, our subconscious mind has one main concern for us... and that is keeping us alive and healthy. Which we learned can also cause us to sabotage our lives out of fear. Our subconscious mind is on a constant quest to heal and integrate our shadow aspects, and it will stop at nothing to accomplish it's mission. This includes attracting us to the very people that will trigger us immensely. We are subconsciously being drawn in to experiencing similar dynamics to that of our childhood if there is still healing that needs to occur. This can be extremely difficult causing us to feel victimized or just like we are unlucky in love or in relationships in general. We will continue to

attract what will heal and integrate our shadow. This can even include highly toxic or abusive relationships. If you find yourself saying things like 'I don't know why I always attract assholes or I don't know why no one at work respects me'... then you have to take a long hard look in the mirror and realize that you and only you (well really your subconscious mind) is attracting in and allowing that abuse as an adult (obviously being abused as a child is a different topic all together.) Now, I don't want to come off as a victim blamer here or insensitive. If you have been victimized in any way, I have deep compassion for you. This is purely about why you might be continuing to experience that as an adult, and discovering if it seems to be a pattern for you. Again, I want to reiterate that this is not pointing fault towards the victim, it's offering a more loving solution to take your power back and break the cycle through healing your shadow. Just remember our subconscious mind just wants us to release our old stuck emotions around our shadow aspects, so it will draw those people to us without our realizing, as an opportunity to heal.. It just wants that shadow aspect inside of us to have it's needs met.

It's important to understand that any stuck or unintegrated negative emotions will literally make you physically ill and cause disease. That's why we experience things such as ulcers, stress induced heart attacks, and also even the advancement of cancer and other illnesses. So... If we keep experiencing a similar toxic pattern in relationships, but never fully heal the shadow aspect of us that caused us to attract that person, then the cycle will continue until we do. Below are some journal prompts to help you uncover your shadow aspects in romantic and family relationships and friendships:

170) What is your relationship like with your immediate family?

_____

_____

171) Who are you closeset to in your family and why?

_____

172) Aside from loved, How do they make you feel?

_____

_____

173) Who are you least closest to and why? How do they make you feel?

_____

_____

174) Do you ever find yourself violating your own boundaries with family or friends or doing things you don't want to do to maintain the relationship?

_____

175) If so, how do you feel when you do this?

_____

176) If you answered yes, how would your relationship be affected if you stopped self sacrificing?

_____

177) Do you think you would lose them or would the relationship suffer if you stopped self sacrificing? If so, How does that make you feel?

_____

178) Why do you choose them over yourself?

_____

_____

179) Do you hold any resentments towards anyone? Why?

_____

_____

180) What is something that is in your power to do to allow you to release that resentment?

_____

_____

181) Think of that person that you resent. Have they experienced anything negative in their lives that could cause them to be that way?

_____

182) Can you think of one good thing about that person that you resent?

_____

183) Do you ever find yourself blaming your parents for certain things in your life now? If so, why?

_____

184) How can you find a way to release them from responsibility and take your power back?

_____

185) Did you pick up any bad habits or traits from your parental figures growing up? Explain.

_____

186) How do you feel when you catch yourself behaving in that way?

_____

187) What small things can you do daily to prevent that behavior?

_____

188) Do you have any repeating patterns or issues with certain family members or friends?

_____

189) If so, what is the pattern? (e.g. my friend would always create drama and guilt me to apologize for things I didn't want to apologize for.)

_____

_____

190) How can you see that you are continuing to participate in this pattern? (e.g. I can see that I apologized even when I didn't believe I should, just to keep peace.)

_____

_____

191) If this pattern doesn't stop, how can you find ways to stop participating in this dynamic? (e.g. I could stand up for myself but that always makes it worse. Or, I could also just stop engaging in the friendship all together.)

_____

_____

192) Can you do this without needing to have your side validated or prove your point? (for example: If I stand up for myself, I would have to get my point across and be understood, but that won't end well, so I have to walk away and accept that I will never prove my point.)

_____

_____

193) What would happen if you cannot have your side validated and understood? (for example: I would have to leave the friendship because I feel like it is abusive.)

_____

_____

194) Can you be ok with not having your point validated? Why or why not?

_____

_____

195) Do you have a deep need to prove your point? if so, why? Where do you think that came from? If that leads your childhood when you were never heard, do the Inner Child Reflections Mediation.

_____

_____

196) What do you value more? Peace or Justice? Why?

_____

_____

197) Do you feel as if you are violating your own boundary by continuing to participate in this dynamic? Or, do you believe they should take full ownership? Explain.

_____

_____

198) Can you find a way to take responsibility? (e.g., Yes, I was violating my own boundary when I apologized for things I didn't do. I can take responsibility and see that is my fault for not standing up for myself.)

_____

_____

199) Does taking responsibility for your participation in this dynamic allow you to feel less resentful? (e.g., Yes, I can see that she got away with what I let her get away with. It was my fault for continuing to allow this behavior.)

_____

_____

200) How will you do better next time? What did you learn?

_____

_____

201) Do you ever blame your parents for certain things in your life now? If so, why?

_____

_____

202) How can you find a way to release them from responsibility and take your power back?

_____

_____

203) Are you happy with the various relationships in your life now? If not, are you doing anything about that and how would you like to see them improve?

_____

_____

204) Do you feel as if you can be your authentic self with most people in your life? If not, who are the people you think would judge you and why?

_____

_____

205) If you beilieve they would judge your authentic self, do you know this to be absolutely true or could you be projecting your own shame about your true self?

_____

206) Who in your life do you admire and why?

_____

_____

207) Who in your life represents love and why?

_____

_____

208) How does the way you treat yourself reflect how other people treat you?

_____

_____

209) Do you believe it is important to put your own needs first or is that selfish, and why?

_____

210) How can you choose yourself and your needs a little more each day?

_____

_____

211) Do you have a self love practice? What are some things that you can do to give yourself more love?

_____

_____

Self love can seem like such an elusive process. Like... 'what am I supposed to do... look in the mirror and say I love you?' YES... do it! I know it can feel weird or inauthentic, but do it anyway... even if you aren't loving yourself. You could treat yourself to something that you've been wanting. You could get dressed up and looking good and compliment yourself, take care of your mind, body, and soul with a healthy diet and commit to daily exercise and a spiritual practice. Focus your attention on the things that you're proud of and not on your short comings. Even if you are in a dark place and are literally hating yourself, it's imperative to your life, if you want any real joy, to do your best to practice self love. We can spend our whole lives looking outside ourselves for love, but we cannot expect to receive healthy love if we don't love ourselves first. That is a void tha t has to be filled by you. Once your own cup is filled to the brim and overflowing with love for yourself, then you can fully give and receive love in a healthy way with another. Life is about relationships, and if you don't love and value yourself, you will attract people that don't love and value you either. Relationships are where we experience the most amount of growth and the most amount of pain in life, so it's so important to clean up what has been stagnant or toxic in your life. If you have any unresolved issues, feelings, guilt, shame, or just grief in relation to another person and resolving it with them is not an option, I reccomend writing a release letter. This is for you and only you, so you can say whatever you want... good or bad and feel free to use any language you want! Whatever makes you feel better. This can also be healing if you have regret about words not said to loved ones that have passed. Just check in with yourself and your heart before you do to make sure that you are ready to face those old wounds. I recommend doing my Heart Opening Meditation before any release letter, and make it a sacred ritual at your altar or sacred space. I also love doing release letters around a full moon and it is a great time for release and transformation. When you feel that you might be finished with the letter, just check in with yourself first by closing your eyes and putting your hand on your heart and intuitively feeling if you are complete. You may find that there is still more there to release. Then when you are complete, burn the letter and release the ashes.

Now, let's talk about some ways that we can take our power back when we are taken over by emotion in relations with other people. it's important to be able to handle your triggers in real time before they handle you and take you to the point that you are on the verge of having an adult temper tantrum! These journal prompts can help us to understand better why we feel triggered and what underlined needs our shadow aspects are desperate to have met so we can integrate those aspects... however, that doesn't mean that we may not ever get triggered again. So, it's important to be able to prevent those intense emotions from snowballing into a full blown adult temper tantrum! I say this jokingly, but it is quite literally what can happen because in those moments when our shadow aspects get triggered, we are reacting from the age that they were supressed into the shadow with the intense emotion that our child selves would have. That's why it can be so hard to control our reactions because we are not thinking with our rational minds. Our 'internal observer' of our own thoughts completely goes out the window when our inner child gets triggered. Often times, the reason we overreact is because we are having a hard time sitting with difficult emotions, and we are looking outside of ourselves to place blame on someone in the hopes that they will make us feel better. Well, often times, this backfires and does quite the opposite... it makes us feel worse. That's because, when we place blame on someone else for the emotions that their actions stirred up inside of us, that can feel like an attack to them. That can cause a counter trigger within them. So, now we have two people that are upset and feel hurt by the other in some way. This is how many relationships fall apart and disagreements can spiral into the pits of blame, shame, and accusation hell! The next time that you catch yourself saying 'you make me feel so unwanted. or unloved or angry' (fill in the blank with any emotion), ask yourself this question "How can anyone make me feel anything?' They can't! It's impossible to make someone feel something. Their actions can stir up those strong emotions inside of you, but you have to take responsibility for those emotions that you are feeling. Everyone reacts differently to things in life, so we can't make assumptions about another's intention.

I will create a hypothetical situation as an example: Let's say Billy's phone dies and he missed all his messages for the day. To Billy's new girlfriend Jessica, an unreturned text could cause her to feel unwanted or unloved, triggering her inner child memories of feeling abandoned waiting for her father to pick her up and take her to the park, but never showing up. Whereas, an unreturned text could cause Billy's last girlfriend to think 'Oh, he must be really busy at work... business must be booming!' In the instance of Billy's new girlfriend Jessica feeling unloved, it could cause her to be cold and distant, act passive/aggressive, withdral her affection and attention, and creating distance in the connection. She could want to play it cool, so she never says anything about the unreturned messages and Billy never knows why she's pulled away. In turn, he feels unwanted and rejected, so he tries to play it cool because he doesn't want to come off as desperate since she's created so much distance. Her pulling away triggers his inner child trauma of being severely bullied in junior high when he asked out his crush and got rejected. Which, in turn, has caused him to create a defense mechanism of playing in cool in romantic relationships out of fear of rejection. That right there is why so many relationships fall apart. Emotional triggers, followed by assumptions, followed by acting from the ego, followed by lack of communication,... resulting in a break up. The unfortunate thing about this example is that niether one of them even realize that they are projecting their shadow's trauma onto the relationship because these feelings and fears are so deeply suppressed into the subconscious shadow. They've probably been approaching all of their relationships in this manner, which could cause them to self sabotage their love live throughout their life time without their knowing. That's really sad when you think about it. Billy and Jessica were crazy about eachother and had a deep connection, but they were acting from their inner child's shadow wounds.

You can see from this story that it would be unfair for Jessica to say 'Billy made me feel unloved.' The truth is Jessica made herself feel unloved because she projected her own childood trauma onto the instance of Billy's phone dying. In this story, Jessica's ego prevented her from even communicating to Billy. However, often times, our inner child getting triggered can have the opposite effect. It can actually cause us to lash out, yell, pout, slam doors, run away, and essentially have an adult temper tantrum. In both instances, we are ruining relationships and making assumptions while blaming others for our negative emotions. I've created a series of questions to ask yourself when you become triggered and feel as if you want to place blame on another person for feeling this way. I will give sample answers below for your understanding.

The next time you feel emotionally triggered by someone and want to either run/pull away or lash out, try to pause before reacting and ask yourself these questions:

- What emotion am I feeling and why?

I am feeling sad and unappreciated because my friend cancelled our plans again. She always does this, and I have done so much for her and she is ungrateful.

- Do I think this person intentionally wanted to cause me to feel ___sad and unimportant___ ?

I don't think she intentionally wanted to hurt me, but she has to know how rude it is to continue cancelling plans, especially after all I've done for her.

(*in the instance of that last question, 99.99% of the time, you will realize that the other person had no malicious intention or desire to cause you to feel bad. Asking that question opens up room for you to look for evidence of why they may have done the thing that triggered you. This allows you to try to understand their perspective a little better. Which can allow you to see that maybe they were just trying to meet their own needs or maybe you were taking it too personally. In the off chance that you believe that they intentionally tried to hurt you, you may be participating in a toxic dynamic. In that case, you have to ask yourself why you continue to allow that, and what need are you getting met by continuing that relationship with them. Once you discover that need, try to find ways to meet that need for yourself. You can also take that topic to the Inner Child Meditation and ask your inner child if you have experienced this same dynamic in the past.)

- Could they have just been trying to meet their own needs by doing the thing that triggered me? If so, what could that need be?

I guess she could've been trying to have her own needs met by cancelling. She mentioned that she was exhausted from work and would be bad company. Maybe she just needed to rest and have some alone time.

- Was there ever a time in my early life that I experienced something similar causing me to feel this way?

Yes, when I was a child my parents would promise to spend time with me and take me places, but they often cancelled because they were tired from work. I made sure to do my homework and clean my room so I had time for them, but they didn't prioritize me. I often felt sad and unimportant. I also felt bad for being upset because I knew they were working so hard.

- Could I be projecting my past onto this scenario?

Maybe I am projecting my past wounds of not feeling valued or important onto this situation. Maybe I am assuming that just because she is tired that means that she doesn't care about me. Maybe I am so frustrated because I am used to feeling bad for wanting to feel important.

If this is an emotional trigger caused from past projections, this series of questions should help you to reach that conclusion and prevent you from sending that nasty text, pouting and running away, yelling, making passive aggressive comments, and just having the good ol' adult temper tantrum! The hardest part of all of this is in the pause before the reaction. Now that you are on your journey of personal development, you can have more awareness when you feel yourself getting triggered. You can call back the conscious observer of your thoughts before you let your inner child run the show, and you can take some time to step away and assess your emotions. The goal is:

TRIGGER $\longrightarrow$ EMOTION $\longrightarrow$ PAUSE $\longrightarrow$ ASK YOURSELF THOSE QUESTIONS $\longrightarrow$ RESPOND

As opposed to TRIGGER $\longrightarrow$ EMOTIONAL OVER REACTION! I will list those questions again on the next page for an easy reference to jot down or remember for those heated moments. Remember, we are not trying to kill our shadow or ego... we are just trying to integrate our shadow and transced our ego. This takes practice and effort!

When you are feeling emotionally triggered, and that emotion is bubbling under the surface ready to explode, remove yourself from the situation. However, it's important to communicate to the other person that you need a moment to yourself. Just fleeing the conversation could be interpreted as abandonment to the other person. Then, PAUSE, close your eyes, put your hand on your heart, take a deep breath, and ask yourself these questions:

- What emotion am I feeling and why?
- Do I think this person intentionally wanted me to feel this way?
- Could they just be trying to meet their own needs? What could that need be?
- Was there a time in my early life that I experienced something similar?
- Could I be projecting?

Now, if this series of questions causes you to feel more enraged or come to a realization that the person is actually intentionally being an asshole, then you have to decide if it is in your best interest to continue a relationship with them. Or, you may have to choose to consciously disengage from the conversation for the time being. If you feel that you do want to come together with this person to have a mutual understanding, then you have a responsibility to communicate your feelings in an open way. Just remember to stay away from those dreaded words 'you make me feel!' If we approach these moments with intention and care, our relationships can actually grow from these tough times, and we can heal our inner child in the process! When we communicate openly and vulnerably, it allows for a sense of humanness and defenses comes down. If you feel as if you need to hold a boundary and remove yourself if you or your loved one is too highly emotionally charged, just remember to make sure you don't just run away. This could cause your loved one to feel disrespected or abandoned in a moment when they might already be feeling some shame. Here are some things that we can say when we are faced with these tough moments:

- 'I'd like to check in with you because I'm feeling a little attacked or hurt by your actions. Can we talk about it?'
- 'I'm actually feeling triggered right now, and I think I need to remove myself from this conversation so I don't overreact. Can we talk about it in a few hours.'
- 'I can see that you are really triggered by this. Is there anything that you need to talk about? How can I help you through this?
- 'I can see that you are really triggered by this. Do you need to take some space and we can talk about this later?'
- 'I can see that you are very upset right now, I'd like to take some time for us to cool off. Can we talk about this tonight?
- 'I am feeling a little (name that emotion) from your actions or words. Can you help me unpack that?

You can see how non-confrontational and vulnerable these responses are. This allows for opportunity, growth, and inner child healing. We just have to remember in the heat of that initial moment TO PAUSE!!! If we can learn to practice this approach, we can learn so much about ourselves and our loved ones. This can catalyze immense growth in our relationships instead of letting a trivial fight potentially cause permanent damage or even end the relationship . So, I will leave you now on this delicate topic of relationships with this lovely quote on the following page.

"Vulnerability is not winning or losing. It's having the courage to show up and be seen when we have no control over the outcome. Vulnerability is not a weakness, it's our greatest measure of courage."

BRENÉ BROWN

The Shadow & Love

Aaaaaah LOVE! My favorite thing in the world! If you haven't already figured it out, relationships are our #1 BIGGEST school in this game called life... especially romantic relationships! They are our biggest mirror to reflect back to us who we are and what we need healed. That is why our subconscious mind is constantly attracting to us the people that will most trigger our shadow's unmet needs. If you are on a path of personal development, this can be extremely helpful in achieving more self awareness and healing. However, if we are just living life on auto pilot and letting our subconscious behaviors run the show, we will not be aware of why we are being so triggered. This is what ruins relationships and causes a lot of shame in those moments of intense reactivity after we get triggered. If you and your partner are both commited to taking accountability for your shadow's wounds and on a path of personal development, you can experience an immense amount of personal growth, deep love, and connection. Your inner child can also experience deep healing through your partner if you both are practicing shadow work with awareness of your triggers. I don't believe that we need to be fully healed in order to attract a healthy partner. I do, however, believe that we have to be practicing self love, be on a path of personal growth, and doing our best to maintain a high vibration. As we know, we attract what we are!

212) On the next page, take a moment to write down what love is to you. Really take your time with this one and give some examples of times you have witnessed love or received it. Write down how it feels, and what it inspires in you. I will leave the entire page for this exercise, so dig deep!

To me, love looks, sounds, and feels like. ..

_____

_____

_____

_____

_____

_____

_____

_____

_____

_____

_____

_____

_____

213) Given your description, do you experience that same love in your romantic relationships?

_____

214) If not, how is it different?

_____

215) When do you feel most loved?

_____

216) Do you enjoy being in romantic relationships or prefer to be single and why?

_____

_____

217) What are some positive things that you believe all of your exes would say about you?

_____

_____

218) Would you agree with those things?

_____

219) What is one major thing that you have learned about yourself from your relationships?

_____

_____

220) Have you ever been in a 'situationship' without commitment, but you really desired true commitment but stayed with the hopes of a future commitment?

_____

221) If so, how did that work out and why did you deny the truth that it was just casual?

_____

_____

222) Or, have you ever stayed in a relationship or 'situationship' longer than you should've? If so, why?

_____

_____

223) What need was being met? Was meeting that need worth staying that long?

_____

_____

224) Where and from what time in your life do you think that need came from?

_____

_____

225) What did you learn from that 'relationship?' How will you do better next time?

_____

_____

226) If you are in a relationship now, are you happy? If not, why are you staying? What needs is your inner child getting met by staying?

_____

_____

_____

227) How can you meet that need yourself and be single? Are you comfortable being single? If not, why?

_____

_____

228) Do you notice any toxic patterns in your romantic relationships? (abuse, control, infadelity, manipulation, co-dependancy, jealousy, fawning, criticism, impatience, ect.) by either you or your previous partners? If so, what are they?

_____

_____

_____

229) If this toxic behavior is done by your partner, why do you continue to accept it? Ask your inner child what need is being met by allowing this treatment? (for example: if my partner is jealous or controlling then I know that he wants me, and I have a deep need to feel wanted and important.)

---

230) What are some things that you could do in your daily life to meet that need yourself? (e.g. I could do things to choose myself every day instead of put other people's needs first to show that I am important to myself.)

---

231) If you are the one engaging in toxic behaviors, ask your inner child 'What is this this behavior protecting me from?' (e.g. if I you are jealous: I am jealous and controlling to protect myself from losing the person I love and ending up alone.

---

232) Then ask your inner child what need it is trying to get met. (for example: I am trying to get my need met of feeling safe. If I know that I am not alone, then I feel safe.)

233) How can you find ways to meet your inner child's need today? (for example: I could do things alone and get more comfortable being by myself and realize that I am still safe on my own.)

234) Do you ever feel jealous of your partner or their life ? If so, why?

235) Are you comfortable being vulnerable with your feelings and needs with your partner? If not, how can you allow yourself to be more vulnerable?

236) Do you typically naturally trust your partners unless they betray you or are you naturally a mistrusting person?

237) If you are mistrusting, why? When did you learn to mistrust in your life? (If anything intense comes up, go to the Inner Child Reflections Meditation.

238) Do you think mistrusting people keeps them from betraying you or do you think it prevents closeness and why or why not?

_____

_____

239) Do you exhibit any negative behaviors in romantic relationships that you wish to change, but have had a hard time changing? Explain.

_____

_____

240) If you answered yes to that question, would you consider that negative behavior to be a coping mechanism like we discussed previously on page 72? (An example of a coping mechanism used in relationships would be defensiveness.) Explain.

_____

_____

241) Let's reference the previous questions #117-122 again with that coping mechanism and answer those series of questions again. They are listed below. To give you a better understanding, I will give the example of defensiveness. The questions are as follows:

So, defensive Sarah... What are you trying to protect me from?

I am defensive because I am protecting you from being wrongly accused for things you didn't do and from looking stupid and losing people's respect. I am protecting you so people don't mistrust what you say and do.

Why would it be so bad for me to expercience

Being wrongly accused, looking stupid, or not trusted?

If you are wrongly accused, you could be punished for things you didn't do. Your partner might think that you're stupid and not trust what you say and do in the future or he might not take you seriously. You could lose people and lose their respect.

At what age did you create this coping mechanism and why?

I probably created this coping mechanism at the age of 6 because my step dad always accused me of things I didn't do and then my mom would punish me. It wasn't fair and I felt like no one believed in me or trusted me. I felt misunderstood and alone.

What unmet needs are driving you to protect me?

My need to be trusted is driving me to protect you by being defensive. I'm scared to be punished for things that aren't true, and for people to stop believing in me and my capabilities. I need to be understood.

What emotion do you feel and why?

I feel frustration that no one understands me and that I always have to prove myself. I feel fear that I will always feel alone and be punished for things I didn't do.

What is something that I can consciously do today to meet your need and make you feel better?

You could start by trusting yourself more and your decisions. You could put yourself out there more in your work and on line, and not worry so much about what people think. You could ask for constructive criticism from loved ones and learn from the feedback instead of take it personally. You could ask yourself the series of questions on page 108 in this book when you are angry with your partner or feeling defensive. You could get comfortable with doing things wrong and see that people still love and respect you. To honor my emotions, you could let yourself cry instead of suppress it, and maybe go for a run to release the frustration. You could honor my emotions by having my feelings witnessed in a safe space with loved ones, or a coach. You could do a meditation to connect to these emotions and move through them.

Do you see how returning to that series of questions can help you to understand why you might keep behaving a certain way towards your parter, even when you don't want to? Once you discover what need you're trying to have met by acting that way, continue to find ways to meet your shadow's need yourself without resorting to that behavior.

242) Do you ever sacrifice your own needs or desires for your partner? If so, why?

_____

_____

243) If so, what would happen if you stopped?

_____

244) Do you fear you would lose them?

_____

245) Is self sacrificing something that you do because you don't want to lose people or because they expect you to?

_____

246) If so, do you harbor resentment or blame them?

_____

247) If so, how can you take responsibility for choosing to self sacrifice?

_____

248) List 2-3 positive traits and 2-3 negative traits about yourself that your current or last partner mirrored back to you. What did you learn about yourself?

_____

_____

_____

249) When you do nice things for your partner do you expect that in return?

_____

250) How would you feel if they never did those nice things back?

_____

_____

251) Do you put expectations on your partner?

_____

252) If so, what are they and do you believe they are fair?

_____

253) What do you believe unconditional love is?

_____

_____

254) Do you think having expectations is unconditional love?

_____

_____

255) Do you believe unconditional love has to be reciprocal?

_____

256) Have you tolerated abuse or poor treatment because of unconditional love?

_____

257) Do you believe that you can still unconditionally love someone, but choose to leave them?

_____

258) How do you feel about commitment or monogamy?

_____

259) Do you feel pressure to settle down or commit because of societal norms or do you desire it?

_____

260) Do you believe that it is more important to love yourself than your partner? Why or why not?

_____

_____

261) If your partner left you with no explanation, would you feel you need a reason or closure, and push them to give you one? Or is the fact that they ghosted you enough to make you want to leave them too?

_____

262) Does having a reason or 'closure' make you feel better about yourself and the rejection?

_____

263) How do you handle rejection?

_____

264) How would it make you feel to be ghosted? Would you feel there is something wrong with you?

_____

265) Do you feel guilt rejecting someone? If so, why?

266) Have you ever stayed longer in a relationship than you wanted out of guilt of hurting someone?

267) If so, why did that other person's feelings matter more than yours?

268) If you grew up with an opposite sex parental figure, describe their persona. Do you find that you are attracted to partners that embody those same qualities?

269) If so, do you think that you have any unhealed wounds around that parental figure that your shadow could be trying to heal through your romantic partners? Like what?

270) How was love given to you as a child? Was it consistent?

271) Do you find that your way of receiving or desiring romantic love is similar to how you received it growing up? Or, is it the complete opposite?

_____

272) Looking back on your relationships, can you identify one good behavior and one negative behavior that you engaged in consistently?

_____

273) What can you learn from that?

_____

_____

274) Give an example from a previous or current relationship when you have felt the most loved.

_____

_____

275) What need did that partner meet to make you feel so loved? How can you find ways to meet that need for yourself?

_____

_____

276) Aside from love, What do you believe is the most important thing in a relationship?

_____

277) What is one thing that you cannot live without in your romantic relationships?

_____

278) On a scale of 1-10, how good do you beleive you are at communicating with your partner?

_____

279) How do you feel about having difficult conversations? Do you avoid conflict?

_____

280) If so, why? How has this affected your relationships?

_____

_____

281) Do you believe avoiding conflict makes things easier and less dramatic or do you believe it can build resentments if you hold it in?

_____

_____

282) Do you feel comfortable freely expressing your needs? If not, why?

_____

283) If not, how can you get more comfortable expressing your needs?

_____

284) Do you ever use sex or affection to get what you want or punish your partner?

_____

285) If you answered yes, how do you think that could affect your sex life with that partner long term?

_____

286) Do you believe that love should feel equal and balanced or do you like to have the upper hand or feel dominated? Explain why.

_____

_____

287) With that last answer in mind, Do you see any connection to your view of dominance in relationships with the way you saw love expressed growing up? Explain.

_____

_____

288) What do you envy/admire in other couples' relationships? Why?

_____

_____

_____

_____

289) Describe what a healthy relationships means to you.

_____

_____

_____

290) Do you find that in your dating life, that you adhere to your own standards of a healthy relationship?

_____

291) If not, what would you like to change?

_____

292) What are some things that are in your control that you can start doing to attract healthier relationships?

_____

_____

293) After answering all of these prompts, can you identify any relationships in your life now or previously that your subconscious shadow could be drawing in for you to experience healing?

_____

294) If so, what need was/is that particular person meeting? (for example: if you keep staying with a controlling partner, maybe you have a deep need to be taken care of.)

_____

295) How can you find ways to meet that need yourself?

296) This is also true for family relationships. Can you identify any difficult family dynamics that you continue participate in just to have your shadow's needs met? (e.g., you could enable your brothers toxic behavior and addictions by loaning him money because you have a deep need to feel connected and valued.)

297) How can you find ways to set boundaries and find other ways to meet those needs?

I will end here with this chapeter on love. In my opinion, romantic relationships provide the most amount of self reflection and contrast required for real growth. It's only through relating with others and observing our reactions that we can truly begin to understand what lies in our shadow. Romantic love leaves us the most vulnerable and raw, and it gives rise to any fears of abandonment we may have. If you have a conscious partner that can embark on this journey of personal development with you, you can both learn so much about yourselves. I have learned through my own difficult lessons in relationships, that we are usually desperately trying to have our partner meet our inner child's needs. This can be very healing when your parnter can offer you that love and support your inner child so desperately needs. However, it is completely unfair to expect your partner to meet all of those needs. Often times, when they can't, this can lead to intense friction. Because, when we are in the heat of the emotional moment, those feelings and inner child traumas that our partner triggers in us, can feel so real and intense. It can feel as if we are experiencing that same old trauma, pain, or abandonment again. Except this time it can be triggered by something as simple as your partner asking you to stack the dishes differently! I also want to be clear when I say 'our partner triggers us', that it is in no way any one else's fault when we get triggered. This can almost sound accusatory as if they are intentionally triggering us or at fault. We must understand that we are responsible for our own triggers. And, we are most certainly responsible for how we respond. If our partner triggers things within us that is reminicent of a deeply painful childhood dynamic, we can literally have an adult temper tantrum. That can look like yelling, silent treatment, slamming doors, or name calling. This is clearly childish behavior. Often times, once we come out of our emotional haze, we can feel deep shame for our reaction. If you have awareness and have been practicing shadow work and personal development, you can take accountability, apologize, and vow to do better next time. If you are lucky enough to have a patient partner, you can both grow together through these tough moments. Conversely, if you are not on a path of personal development, you can be completly cluelss as to how you are projecting your shadow aspects onto your partner. Often times, we will continue to beat an issue to death since the painful emotions can feel so real to us. We can argue and break our partner down to admit fault just to have our inner child validated. This is how relationships can become toxic and manipulative. Sadly, relationships are unknowingly ruined, and we just chalk it up to 'oh we just weren't compatible or 'he was an asshole.' If we don't take accountability and make the changes necessary to be a healthy loving partner, we will continue to expreience these same dynamics throughout our lives. That's why it is so important to do shadow work and heal your inner child. Don't make that your partner's responsibility. Integrate those shadow aspects into your conscious personality and you will open up your life to create beautiful, healthy, loving relationships!

✦ Shadow Work + Forgiveness ✦

Once you start actively practicing shadow work, you have a greater awareness of all the ways that you are projecting your subconscious traumas onto other people. It's a beautiful thing because you can start to check yourself from overreacting. The other amazing thing that happens is, that you begin to see all the ways that other people are projecting as well. Obviously we don't truly know what's going on in other people's subconscious minds, but if we know them well enough, we can see how they might be projecting. Now I don't want to exuse people for nasty or poor behavior, but when we can understand this, it helps us to have more compassion for them. It makes it easier to see that the nasty thing that they are doing or saying to us isn't even about us at all. It's about them. It's usually their wounded inner child lashing out just like we used to do before we started our shadow work process. This can help us to not take things so personally anymore. The other benefit of doing shadow work, is that this allows us to practice forgiveness and understanding in our lives much easier. To be able to forgive someone that has hurt you is the most freeing feeling, and it is truly spiritually transformative. Something happens when we are able to truly forgive those that have trespassed against us. It's like we uplevel spiritually. We crack the code and beat this level we are stuck at in this video game called life! I have a great analogy about what happens when we are about to up level in our life. It goes like this: Whenever we are about to make a shift in our consciousness and up level to our next stage of life, we will encounter a big scary monster. It's like the monster at the end of the level of a video game. Once you have made it all the way to the end of your level, you are faced with a monster. Once you slay that monster, you can move up to the next level. When you get to the next level, you usually gain more powers and tools and tokens to fight the bad guys and save the princess. The same is true for life. With great progress comes great challenge. Often times that big scary monster that's preventing us from up leveling is just past resentments or anger that we are harboring against others or just against life in general. That monster is just something that we have to forgive if we want to make it to the next level. Those tools and tokens that we receive for slaying that monster are peace, love, understanding, and compassion. Those tools are priceless, and they are what you need to win the game! And, do you want to know the beautiful, amazing thing about that? All we have to do is drop all of our weapons, stop fighting so hard, stop hurting ourselve and just let go. Look that monster in the eye and say I forgive you.... and POOF! Just like that, the monster disappears and you can easily make your way to the next level. You can take your time and enjoy the journey. On the other hand however, if you don't lay down your armor and forgive that monster, you will be fighting him forever, end up broken and bruised and never even make it to the next level... let alone rescue the princess! Do you get where I'm going here with this analogy? Forgiveness is not only your key to freedom, but it is also your key to acheiving complete success. Some people might say 'I forgive, but I won't forget!' Well, I hate to break it to ya, but that is not true forgiveness. That is just your ego seeing forgiveness as a weakness and trying to find a way to punish someone with your anger while still being the suffering victim. Well, do you know what happens when we continue to identify as the victim? We will continue to attract people that victimize us. Life will reflect back to us exactly what we claim it to be. If somewhere inside of you, you believe that forgiveness equals weakness or to forgive means that your perpetrator has won in some way, then you do not see the true power that you hold when you forgive. It is actually the most courageous thing that you can do. It's choosing your own peace over the need to be right or the need to impart justice on another. Just think about it like this... forgiveness is truly a gift that you give to yourself. Do it not because they deserve the forgiveness, but rather because you deserve the peace. The great thing about learning about the shadow, is that you can better spot when other people are projecting from their wounds. You can better see the origins of thier cruelty, and feel a sense of compassion. To be able to do this is to transcend the ego. I could go on and on about the power of forgiveness, but I hope you get it! It is your golden ticket to freedom. So, let's explore more to find what monsters might need slaying in your life with these journal prompts on the following pages!

298) Have you ever been conditioned to believe that forgiveness is weakness or letting the other person win?

_____

299) Do you believe in the statement 'forgive but don't forget? Why or why not?

_____

_____

300) Is there anyone in your life that you haven't truly forgiven? If so, why?

_____

_____

301) What emotion do you feel when you think about what this person did? What can you do to move through and release that emotion?

_____

302) Have you ever self medicated to ease the pain of resentment and anger towards another? Did that take away the pain? Were there consequences?

_____

_____

303) Do you ever find yourself playing out scenarios in your mind telling off the people that have done you wrong? Do you ever fantasize about what you wish you would've said or done? Explain.

_____

_____

304) If so, does it feel good to mentally let them have it? How does that make you feel? Does that negative energy go away or is it magnified?

_____

305) Have you ever forgiven someone in the past, but they continue to trespass against you or hurt you?

_____

306) If so, how did that make you feel? Did you lose trust in them? Do you continue to allow them to violate your trust?

_____

_____

307) If so, did it make you lose trust in other people?

_____

308) Have you ever punished people in your life for things other people did to you? (e.g. mistrusting your current partner because your ex cheated)

_____

309) If so, do you think that is fair? Does it provide any punishment to the person that actually hurt you? Is it negatively affecting your current relationships?

_____

_____

310) Do you struggle with harboring any anger or resenments towards your parental figures? If so, for what?

_____

311) If so, how has that resentment you harbor affected your life?

_____

312) Are they are aware of the thing that you resent them for or do you keep this to yourself? If so, why?

_____

313) Do you struggle with forgiving yourself?

_____

314) If so, what are you not forgiving yourself for and why?

_____

315) Do you withhold self forgiveness as a form of punishing yourself for something you did?

_____

316) Do you believe forgiving yourself or someone else would excuse the bad behavior? Does that prevent you from forgiving?

_____

317) Can you think of a time when someone forgave you for something that you did that you felt shame about? How did that make you feel?

_____

318) Have you ever tried to forgive someone but just couldn't let it go? Why do you think that is?

_____

_____

319) Have you ever thought that you had forgiven someone, but then old resentments creep up? Why?

_____

_____

320) Have you ever claimed to forgive a partner, but throw things back in their face when you have a fight?

_____

321) If so, how did it affect your relationship?

_____

_____

322) If you feel a sense of betrayal from someone close to you and they sincerely apologize, can you truly forgive or does the relationship feel permanently damaged?

_____

323) Have you ever felt a sense of betrayal as a child? Explain.

_____

_____

_____

324) if so, how did it feel and how has it affected your life and your relationships?

_____

_____

325) Recall the last time that you had to forgive someone. Looking back, do you believe that you truly whole heartedly forgave them?

_____

_____

326) If not, why are you harboring resentments? What emotions did their actions trigger inside of you?

_____

_____

327) If there are any people that you have had a hard time forgiving, reflect on why that may be, and ask yourself if they had triggered any of your inner child's shadow aspects? If so, in what way?

_____

_____

If we want to free ourselves from the shackles of intense anger and resentments that are poisoning our mind, body, and spirit, then we have to get comfortable with the idea of trying to find the good in the bad. This can be so difficult for people that have experienced extreme abuse or tragic loss. Many times there is literally no light that we can find in such darkness. If the pain is too deep, you can start by acknowledging that this pain has lead you down a path of self discovery and personal development. If you're here reading this, then you are trying to improve your life, and in doing so, you get to meet parts of yourself that you never knew existed. You have been propelled towards a path of healing and self development, which is an accomplishment in and of itself. So many people just spend their lives living like zombies in the matrix never even exploring the juciness of life, but here you are! You are doing the work, so kudos to you! It's so crucial to our healing process that our suffering must not be in vain. We have to find a way to rise up from the ashes and turn tragedy into triumph, and sometimes that means accepting the apology that we might never actually receive. We have to choose forgiveness. In doing so, they no longer have control over us. We take our power back. Then we can even alchemize that suffering into resilience and share our story with other people to help them heal their suffering.

328) Think of the worst thing that anyone has ever done to you, can you dig deep and find one lesson that you learned from it to take away? If so, what did you learn?

_____

_____

_____

329) Can you find anything in their personal history that they may have experienced that could've caused them to behave that way to you? Explain.

_____

_____

330) If so, can you forgive them more easily? Or maybe even have compassion for them?

_____

331) Looking back at the times that you have been betrayed, have any of those been times when you had poor boundaries and allowed that behavior? Explain.

_____

_____

332) If so, how can you take responsibility now?

_____

Often times, the pain that we feel and anger that we hold inside of us just needs to be witnessed and validated. Many of us have a deep need to have our feelings validated, myself included. This can come from a childhood wound of never feeling heard or understood. This is very common. I see this need playing out in my life whenever I have an argument with my partner. Most times I don't need him to apologize and take ownership, I just desperately need him to validate my feelings and say, 'Ok babe, I see how that could be hurtful, but that was not my intention.' This is literally the antidote to my suffering right there. So, when we are harboring resentments towards others, it can be very healing to get your feelings validated. When we can't receive this from the perpetrator, we can receive this from trusted friends and support groups. Sometimes, just sharing our story and receiving validation and compassion is all we need to let it go. Once, we are able to let it go, we can no longer identify as a victim. This is hard for many people that have suffered abuse because they literally identify as the victim. This can be difficult because once they drop their victim story, they don't know who they are without it. As we already know, we attract what we are, so it's time to just let that poison go. It's just not worth it. I hate to sound insensitive, but it's just the truth. I say this with a heart full of love and compassion... stop suffering and take your power back. Find a way to gain resilience and strength from your hardships and go be a bad ass! Don't let it harden your heart, but rather break it open to fearlessly share your love with the world. By holding onto anger and resentments, you are literally allowing this person or situation to continuously have power over your life and keep you at a vibration to attract more suffering. When it comes to things like forgiveness, surrender, and letting go of attachments, they can feel like these elusive concepts or practices. We can desire with all of our hearts to be able to surrender or forgive, but have a hard time understanding how. This requires continuous effort. That is why we call it a practice. As long as we are living this human existence, our ego will continue to bring up these negative feelings and fears to try to protect us. We just have to continue our practice of surrender... which requires love. And if you can't find it in your heart to do it out of love for the person that betrayed you, then do it out of love for yourself. If you are having a hard time letting go or you feel resentment towards another rise up inside of you, Try this following exercise:

Stop and take a few deep breaths and put your hand on your heart and ask yourself these questions:

- Does this anger that I am holding right now have any affect on the person I am holding it against?
- Does this anger I feel bring justice to what they did to me or others or does it just live inside of me?
- What affect does this anger have on me and my relationships?
- Who is this anger hurting worse... me or them?
- Am I willing to allow them to continue to have power over my state of being?
- What did I learn from this situation and how can it make me better?
- How can I choose to love myself enough to let go of this poison inside of me?

When you reflect on your answers to those questions, you can truly see that holding resentments is only hurting you. After these series of questions, you can state the following affirmation while holding an image this person or people in your mind:

'I forgive you for what you have done and I release my desire to seek justice because I know that all is balanced in the karmic wheel of life. I send you love, and in doing so, I love myself and set myself free.'

This is how you take your power back. And if you really want to make that suffering actually serve you, then you have to do your best to look for some kind of silver lining and find a lesson in the pain. If you can do that, then you can add a little more to that affirmation by adding these words with this person in mind:

"Thank you for the lesson. This suffering was not in vain.'

When we practice forgiveness, and always look for the blessing in the lesson, something amazing happens... we are literally training ourselves to see the good in the bad. When we get good at strengthening our forgiveness muscle, that translates into other areas of life as well. We become better able to take life's setbacks with grace. We can look at our losses, setbacks, and misfortunes with curiosity about what we can learn. With time and practice, we can even be grateful for the misfortune as it has catalysed our growth.

If you are struggling with forgiving yourself, then you can take a few deep breaths, put your hand on your heart and ask yourself:

- How does this resentment I have towards myself feel right now?
- Does holding this anger towards myself make amends for what happened?
- What affect does this emotion have on me and my relationships?
- What can I learn from this experience or regret?
- What are some positive things I can do everyday to balance the karmic wheel of life?
- If I hurt someone, what could I do in my daily life to make them proud?
- How can I choose to love myself enough to let go of this poison inside of me?

Now you can see by your answers again, that holding on to this guilt serves no purpose at all. So now, with your hand over your heart say the following affirmation: (I highly suggest doing this while looking in the mirror and speak to yourself directly.)

'I forgive myself for what I have done and I release my need to make amends by punishing myself. I choose to balance the karmic wheel of life by choosing to do my best going forward. I deeply love and forgive myself and in doing so, I set myself and any others that were hurt free. I am grateful for this lesson'

(If you are doing mirror work you would speak to yourself directly by saying 'i forgive you...')

This practice is so important because as we know, what we are feeling internally attracts what we experience externally. If we feel deep shame or guilt, we will never live a full abundant life. When we can love and forgive ourselves, we are nuetralizing that negative energy around this thing, and setting everyone involved free. When we use the lesson that we learned to become a better person instead of just feeling guilt and shame, we make the other person's suffering not be in vain. That is how you make amends. This is also a good time to write a release letter to yourself or anyone in your life that you are struggling to forgive or that you wish to forgive you or make amends with. Whenever you are writing a release letter, it is always for you and you only, so feel free to go all out. Cuss those people out if you have to! Express your deep anger and maybe even scream into a pillow and give it a few good punches! Do whatever you have to to let those emotions go. As always, when you are done, check in with yourself to see if you feel complete. When it feels right, burn the letter and release the ashes. I could go on and on about the empowering freedom that true forgiveness gives, but I will leave you with this famous quote instead...

"Holding resentments is like drinking poison and expecting the other person to die."

UNKNOWN

The Shadow + Money

How do you feel about your relationship with money? This question can be very tricky because our conscious mind can be telling us 'We want money!', but our subconscious mind could be sabotaging that for a variety of reasons. How easily we attract money is dependant on our fears, our faith, our feelings of worthiness, our attitude towards spending, our programmed beliefs about money, our unhealed traumas, our daily vibration, and so much more! YIKES! Why is money so important anyway? The obvious answer to that is... 'we need it to live, duh!' Well, at the core of that is security. We need it to feel safe and secure. We need it to survive. If we grew up in a home that felt unsafe, that could program us to feel a deep need for security. Even if we grew up feeling financially secure, if we didn't feel physically secure or safe, it can imprint us with a deep fear of unsafety. An unsafe childhood might lead to an obsession with a need to feel safe and secure in our adult life. That could cause us to have a major fear imprint around money. And we all know that what we resist persists. So, if we are feeling fear... that is just a resistance to accepting what is and wanting to control an outcome. That will completley block you from the free flow of money and abundance. Sure, you can work hard for your entire life, make a decent living, and invest your little earnings in a side hustle or real estate and make your little extra cash for retirement, BUT you may never be a magnet for effortless wealth. You could work hard your whole life and arrive at retirement resentful that you didn't enjoy life more. We know that everything is energy, right? Well, that includes money. We attach so much energy to money. We project our shadow's judgements onto money just as we do to people. The amazing thing about doing shadow work and inner child healing, is that it affects your life in every other area. In ways you never expected... and that includes attracting abundance. So, let's dive in and see what we can discover about your own subconscious money imprint!

333) Did you feel financially secure and safe growing up?

_____

334) Did you feel physically safe in your home growing up? Were you physically or emotionally attacked?

_____

335) Did you ever feel unsafe in general for any reason growing up?

_____

_____

336) Does money equal safety to you in your adult life?

_____

337) If so, do you find yourself wanting to control the area of money in your life? Do you feel fear around money?

_____

338) What was the attitude around money in your home growing up?

_____

339) Did you grow up hearing negative statements regarding money? (e.g., 'money is the root of all evil' or 'nothing good ever comes easy' or 'you shouldn't care about money.')

_____

If you have a fear around money and feeling safe, try to get into a habit of comforting yourself and your inner child when you are feeling moments of fear around money or security and safety in general. If you feel resistance to paying bills or you are spending with anxiety... stop and take a few deep breaths. You can put your hand on your heart and say: 'You are ok, you are safe, you are taken care of, everything will be ok, you have everything you need.' Ground and center yourself and release that resistance to allow the current of money energy to flow more freely to you. That is why money is called 'currency'... it is a current meant to flow freely and with ease.

340) How were taught to value money or things? (Often times, if you grow up without money, you value it so much that you may want to hoard it and not spend it. Or, the opposite can happen if you grow up spoiled. You may not appreciate the value of things if they are always handed to you.)

_____

_____

341) How old were you when you got your first job? How did you feel about your first check and what did you do with it? Does that reflect the way you feel about money and spend as an adult (a personal story: I got my first job as a waitress in a diner when I was 14. I will never forget my first day counting tips feeling so excited stacking my $1 bills on the floor. I will never forget... there was 61 of them! All I wanted to do was spend it on something cute for myself and for the people I love and keep making more of it!

_____

_____

_____

This attitude towards money carried over into my adult life... to a fault. I was on a hamster wheel of work hard, spend hard. Money would flow in and out like water. I can see when I reflect on that, that earning money equaled hard work. If I were to have to work so hard, then I should at least have cute things or fun experiences. This mindset created a money shadow of wealth = hard work. Furthermore, I learned that money was fleeting because I spent it so recklessly, and I didn't appreciate the value of it. Knowing my money imprint allows me to shift that mentality and energy earning and maintaining money.

342) Are you comfortable receiving money just as a gift without feeling indebted?

_____

343) Do you provide a service or sell anything? If so, do you charge your worth or often give 'deals?'

_____

344) How do you spend money? with ease and excitement, recklessly, or with hesitation or caution?

_____

345) Do you believe that you deserve wealth? Why or why not?

_____

_____

346) Are you jealous of people with money or people who seem to attract money easily?

_____

347) Do you feel happy for people who win money or achieve success in making a lot of money easily or do you feel resentful?

_____

348) Do you ever feel a sense of unfairness in regards to your having or receiving of money?

_____

349) Do you believe that you have to work hard to make or deserve money?

_____

350) Do you believe that money is energy?

_____

351) Do you beleive that your attitude towards it and how you treat it affects how you will receive it?

_____

352) Do you love money?

_____

353) Do you believe that it is bad or greedy to love or deeply desire money?

_____

354) How can you get more comfortable loving money?

_____

355) Do you pay your bills with resistance or enthusiasm?

_____

356) Do you ever say things like 'I can't afford that right now' or 'I wish I could, but I don't have the money, or 'I am so broke!"?

_____

357) If so, do you believe that speaking that way can block your abundance and reinforce those limiting beliefs you hold about money?

_____

358) When was the last time you splurged and bought something nice or treated yourself to something special?

_____

359) How did it feel? Did you feel any guilt splurging on yourself? If so, why?

_____

360) Would you consider yourself a generous person?

_____

361) What does being generous mean to you?

_____

362) If you can't afford to be generous with your money, can you find other ways to be generous?

_____

363) How can you do that?

_____

_____

364) When was the last time you invested money on self improvement of your mind/body/soul?

_____

365) What are your dreams/goals? (dream job, amount of money, dream home and goals, ect.)

_____

_____

366) Do you believe your goals and dreams are realistic?

_____

367) If not, why?

_____

368) What could you be doing more of to meet those goals and dreams?

_____

_____

369) What emotion do you feel when you talk about money? (e.g.,: stress, excitement, fear, dread, gratitude, etc.)

_____

370) If that emotion is negative, how can you find a way to make it positive? When was a time money made you feel light and happy?

_____

371) Do you want to experience financial wealth and freedom?

_____

372) If so, why? What would you do with it?

_____

_____

_____

373) How would that make you feel? List 3 emotions that you would feel if you had complete financial freedom now.

_____

_____

374) Do you believe that you need money to feel those things?

_____

375) How can you find ways to feel those things every day even now without financial abundance?

_____

_____

_____

To give you an example, financial freedom would make me feel peace, relief, and excitement. If I am living every day stressed about money, then I am not feeling peace, and I will NEVER be a vibrational match to receive money. If I dread paying my bills, than I am resisting the flow of money energetically leaving my bank account. How can I expect money to flow back to me energetically? I have to find ways every day to already experience those feelings that I believe that money will bring me. Some ways I could feel peace is through meditation and music or going to the beach or walking in nature. I can feel a sense of relief by setting a small goal and accomplishing it. I can make a list of annoying little chores I've been avoiding and check things off to feel the relief of getting them done. I can feel excitement through dance and play in my every day life. I can make free things feel exciting and extravagant. I could go on a picnic with my partner and drink cheap champagne while we toast to having all our dreams come true. We have to work ourselves into that place of excitement to be a vibrational match to receive money.

If you want to be a magnet for abundance you have to find small ways to feel those emotions even now without the financial freedom. You have to find ways to feel grateful for whatever it is that you have right now. Even if it's not much. If it's hard to feel blessed at this time in your life, give thanks for living to see another day. Or for your dog that loves you unconditionally. Feeling abundant in every now moment and expressing gratitude for it is the fastest path to abundance... along with taking inspired action, of course! This is LITERALLY the secret to manifesting ANYTHING in life. I cannot say enough how important this concept is to grasp. It's not easy... trust me, I know! Fear can take over so easily when we are not truly experiencing financial abundance, BUT we to search our lives to find ways to celebrate the abundance that we do have. That can keep us in that vibrational realm to receive more.

Hopefully these journal prompts can shed some light on your relationsip with money, and give you a better understanding of how you may have even been preventing it from flowing freely into your life. Below are some things you can practice if you have a dense money shadow.

- Start getting exciting about paying your bills instead of feeing dread. Give thanks for your cell phone when you pay your phone bill and for the comfort you feel from the A/C when you pay your electric bill.

- When you are tipping your waitress or paying your hairstylist, imagine all the ways that your money will enhance their life and feel proud and happy to give your money.

- Start treating yourself to nice things, services, or experiences on occasion and remind yourself that you are worthy of having money to buy nice things. Dress up fancy and play the part of wealth!

- Be generous as often as you can. If you can't be generous with money, be generous with your time, compliments, and love!

- Take note of any limiting beliefs you have about money, and consciously change those statements. (e.g., Instead of saying things like 'I am too broke to buy what I want', say something like, 'I wonder how I will buy that thing that I want.' (Allow yourself to get excited thinking about it!)

- If you have any strong negative emotions around money, take that feeling to my Emotion Reflections Meditation.

- If you have strong negative programming around money or safety that you learned from your childhood caregivers, take that to the Inner Child Reflections Meditation and reprogram that belief

- Start LOVING money! Tell it you love it, invite it to come into your life. Talk to it sweetly and keep it organized nicely in your wallet. I even keep a little money on my altar as well. Spend with enthusiam and deep gratitude for the money you have, knowing that it will flow right back to you.

- Allow yourself to receive anything and everything from money to gifts to favors to energy and time. Decide that you are worthy of receiving without having to reciprocate.

- Spend money on things that will enhance your growth like personal development, coaches, mentors, or classes. Invest in yourself because you are worthy.

- NEVER focus on what you don't have. ALWAYS practice gratitude for what you do have.

- Never spend money with guilt or hesitation.

- Don't hoard your money or be too tight with it. That puts out an energy of lack and not having enough and that's what you will attract.

- Be smart, but use your intuition and not your fears to maintain a responsible balance of spending and saving.

- Get aquainted with the idea that money is just energy and choose to see it as always flowing freely towards you. Get comfortable allowing it to flow out. This keeps the energy of money moving and flowing back to you.

- If you provide a service or sell something, charge your worth! NEVER give aways freebies or hook people up out of obligation. Only do it if you really want to gift them something.

- Realize that everything good in your life from the food that you eat to the sunshine IS abundance. Money is not the only thing that equals abundance. You have wealth now!

- Try not to barter your services instead of receive payment. This sends a message to the Universe that you can't afford to pay for things and have to offer up your services. This can keep you in a lack mentality. Instead of barter, just both pay eachother for the value of your service.

- Donate your money or give to charity with enthusiasm. This will literally multiply your abundance.

- Last but not least, practice non attachment when you invest your money or gamble. Get comfortable with the idea of loosening your grip on it.

Ask yourself everyday... How can I feel rich without money?

The Attitude of Gratitude

So, I fianlly have some good news after all this intense healing you've been doing! For all the ways I have spoken about how the subconscious mind is out to sabotage our lives, it is equally a magical tool that we can use and re-program to suit our needs and attract our conscious desires! The first thing that I will discuss in re-trianing your brain and shifting your reality is my favorite thing in the whole world..... drum roll please....

Gratitude!!!

We literally cannot be in a low vibration while we are practicing gratitude. I won't go too in depth about the importance of gratitude as I believe that it is pretty obvious. Gratitude can release toxic emotions and ease the pain of envy as well as reduce anxiety. If we begin to train our brain to look for things to be grateful for everyday, then we will find them wherever we look and we will attract more in. As we learned in the last chapter, we have to BE what we want to attract. If we want to be abundant, but we are poor, then we have to find ways to feel abundant. How can we do that... gratitude! Even if you don't have an abundance of money, or health, or romantic love, you can look around your life and see so much abundance all around you. You can feel grateful for the abundance of sunshine, beautiful scenery, or delicious food. Amazing things to feel grateful for are all around us... we just have to look for them and give thanks. That is all you need to get into alignment and become a vibrational match to your heart's desires. When we have a shadow work practice and work on releasing old emotions, we can let go of old resentments and open our life up to seeing all the beauty around us instead of feeling vicimized and reliving our past traumas. We can take our power back and be grateful for the lessons and the strength it gave us!

In the following questions, reflect with a grateful heart and really give thanks for your answers.

376) What are you most grateful for about your life?

_____

_____

_____

377) What are you most grateful for about your personality or character? (Remember, no one will see this. This is for you and only you... so go for it and give yourself thanks!) Don't be humble!

_____

_____

_____

378) What material possessions are you grateful for?

_____

_____

379) What is a physical attribut (s) that you are grateful for?

_____

380) What is a natural gift (s) or talent that you posses that you are grateful for?

_____

_____

381) Who are you grateful to have in your life and why?

_____

_____

_____

_____

382) What are you most grateful for from your child hood and why? If you can't find anything to be grateful for, than what lesson that you took from it can you be grateful for?

_____

_____

383) What is one thing you are grateful for about today?

_____

384) What is one opportunity that you were given that you are grateful for?

_____

385) What is one relationship that is over, but you are grateful that you experienced it and why?

_____

386) What are you grateful for about the role that you play in your daily life (job, school, parenting or home life?)

_____

_____

387) What is one lesson that you are grateful for that you had to learn through heartbreak or trauma?

_____

_____

388) What is one strength you are grateful for that you gained through adversity?

_____

389) What is one obstacle that you had to overcome that you are grateful for because it taught you something new?

_____

390) What is one rejection you are grateful for because looking back you see you dodged a bullet or you found something better?

_____

391) What is one challenge or loss that you are grateful for because it taught you to value something important that you took for granted?

_____

392) Think of the worst thing that you have ever experienced in your life. Dig deep, and find something to be grateful for in experiencing that tragedy.

_____

_____

_____

"*Gratitude is riches. Compliant is poverty*"

DORIS DAY

Affirmations

Now, I'm not saying that we can 'love and light' our way to happiness with gratitude and affirmations! However, as we know, shadow work can be intense and bring up many negative emotions, so we have to bring in some love and light as well to balance the energies and just feel good! Positive affirmations are also a good way to retrain your subconscious mind. But, remember that our subconscious mind communicates to us through feelings. So, if your affirmation is 'I am confident', but you really feel insecure, then your affirmation won't work. Try to rephrase your I am statements with phrases like 'I wonder how I am confident in my life.' Your subconscious mind doesn't understand past or future. It only operates in the present, so it's imortant to claim I AM in the now as if it's already there. By saying the words 'I wonder how I AM confident', you are giving your subconscious mind a way to search for those things, thus attracting it to you while still claiming I AM. If we say 'I will be confident', that is reinforcing that we are not now. So, that affirmation just attracts more of the longing for confidence without actually attracting it. Also, we feel less resistance to believing the I AM statement when we start by saying 'I wonder.

'Another great way to attract something in is to say 'wouldn't it be nice if....? 'Wouldn't it be nice to get that job.' or 'Wouldn't it be nice if I got a raise.' This statement has a playful energy that allows your subconscious mind to search for ways to draw that thing to you. There is really no resistance when we say "wouldn't it be nice. It's This gives an air of mystery and excitement.

393) List 3 'I wonder how I am' affirmations. Try to use one of the traits you envied about other people in the previous exercises. For example:

I wonder how I am confident
I wonder how I am successful
I wonder how I am strong

_____

_____

_____

In this instance. I am sure that my subconscious mind can find at least one thing that I am confident about, successful at, and one way that I am strong. Allow your subconscious mind to look for those things that you wrote down. Affirm it, release it, and don't worry about it on a conscious level. This allows your subconscious mind to look for the evidence and call more in. Get it? It doesn't have to make sense to your conscious mind. It just has to give your subconscious mind something to look for and something to attract. And, it has to be stated in the present moment. So, don't say 'I wonder how I WILL BE successful. That just encourages your subconscious mind to think that you will be someday, but not now. It's also important to remember that just like the subconscious mind doesn't understand time like past and future, it also doesn't differentiate from positive or negative. It is completely objective and it only understands the object that you are focusing on. So, if you claim something like 'I do not want to lose my job, the only thing it understands is 'lose my job.' So, you have to get used to claiming things in the positive. So, instead, you would say 'I am grateful to keep my job. '

It's also important to do your best to avoid the word 'want'. It sends the message to your subconsious mind that you don't already have it. So replacing 'I want' with 'I am grateful to have' is more effective. This is all very important because our subconscious mind is literally magnetizing to us what we feel, who we are, what we believe, AND what we need to heal. So, learning to work will the subconscious mind will improve your life in all areas.

Now, think of a few things you would like to create or manifest. Write 3 'wouldn't it be nice if....' statements. (e.g., wouldn't it be nice if I sold a lot of books? Wouldn't it be nice if I won the contest?)

_____

_____

_____

_____

Do you notice how little resistance there is in these statements? Approaching manifesting in this way gives your subconscious mind something to get excited about and attract in. It also allows your conscious mind to fantasize and imagine it in a more playful way. There is no attachment to an outcome with this kind of statement. Try it in your everyday life, and notice how playful and relaxed it feels!

Conclusion

Welp, if you made through this entire journal and completed all these tough questions, I congratulate you, my friend! Thank you for investing in this workbook and trusting in me to take you on this journey. This process of self discovery and being totally raw, real, vulnerable, and honest with yourself is not for the feint of heart. It is my deepest wish that you learned a few things about yourself and experienced some healing along the way. So, I will leave you with these last few journal prompts to reflect on this journey.

394) Through doing this work, did you get to know parts of yourself on a deeper level, and do you feel more connected to yourself? In what ways?

_____

_____

_____

395) Did you gain what you intended from this book?

_____

396) Do you love and accept yourself more now?

_____

If you received even half of the breakthroughs that I experienced in writing this book, then your life will be transformed. As I have said many times in this book, please be gentle with yourself as you walk down this path of personal transformation and growth. Often times when we are healing, we can feel a deep sense of guilt or shame for our past behaviors because now we are able to see our past selves from our new higher perspective. We have already learned that guilt and shame serves no one. Please always remember that. All one can do to make amends is to make a vow to it's former self to make it proud by being the best version of you that you can possibly be moving forward. I am so very proud of you for committing to this journey of self improvement, and I hope you are proud of yourself too. I pray that you can leave this experience with some tools to continue your journey of self development, along with a deeper love, compassion, and understanding for yourself and the world around you. While you are doing the work, making the changes, and slaying those monsters as you up level in life, please remember to play along the way. All this work we have done with our inner child calls for us to find ways to express that child's need to enjoy this experience of life and express who it really is. So please dance, and laugh, and take the long way home just to hear the rest of the song. Eat the delicious food and tell everyone just how much you love them. Please revel in awe at the beauty of the setting sun and the sound of the ocean. Don't take this life and yourself so seriously as much as humanly possible, and please remember to be kind to your fellow humans We are all on this delicate, difficult, wild and beautiful journey of life together, and we have to support each other as brothers and sisters. It is my deepest passion to see this world come together in love and understanding, and I beleive with my whole heart that if we each do our part in healing ourselves, then we can heal this planet. I truly believe that with each soul that slays those monsters and up levels their life by doing this work, the collective consciousness of this planet rises higher. So keep up the good work beautiful soul... I am rooting for you! I know that you will step into all of your greatness and make the very best out of this juicy, delicious, wild, and beautiful experience of life!

Many thanks to you for letting me be a part of your magnificent journey... it is truly an honor. As always, I am here to hold space, guidance, and support if you are interested in one on one coaching.

You can visit my website for more information at www.consciousreflectionscoaching.com or scan the QR code below. And please sign up for my newsletter to stay up to date with all of my workshops and offerings!

It is with great love and pride that I leave you now. HAPPY INTEGRATING... I love you!

"Your entire experience of this life is just a reflection of the light and dark inside of you. What do you want reflected back to you when you look into the mirror of your life?"

SARAH SATRE

Made in the USA
Las Vegas, NV
19 October 2024

10075943R00098